She Writes for Him

Stories of
Living
Hope

Debbie —
 Thank you for including me
in your prayers (at Karla's request)
I appreciate it very much ☺
 Kind regards,
  J. Elizabeth Renich
  (chapter 4)
 Psalm 20:5 | March 2021

She Writes for Him

Stories of
Living
Hope

ROMANS 8:28
BOOKS
AN IMPRINT OF **REDEMPTION**
PRESS

FEATURING BEST-SELLING AUTHORS
LIZ CURTIS HIGGS
PAM FARREL
DEBBIE ALSDORF

Dedication

She Writes for Him: Stories of Living Hope is dedicated to all women who have suffered immeasurably from cancer to abuse and who have trusted the only One who is able to sustain us in the middle of a terrible storm.

These are the brave stories of women who have emerged from their dark places, whole and full of life, willing to speak the truth so others can find healing.

Cynthia Cavanaugh
Managing Editor

TABLE OF CONTENTS

She Writes for Him
Stories of Living Hope

Part 2: *Addiction*

Part 3: *Abuse*

Part 4: *Mental Health*

Part 5: Suffering

Introduction

In May 2019 I was driving home from the Northwest Christian Writers Renewal with the top down on my convertible, the sun out, and the mountains in view, when God gave me a vision. He dropped the name "She Writes for Him" into my heart, and I somehow knew it would start as a book compilation, then a podcast, then a bootcamp or writers' retreat, and finally a conference. Like an unfolding daydream, this was the vision God cast before me on that gorgeous spring day.

I knew it wouldn't be stories on random topics, but rather it would be women sharing their pain, their suffering, and how God helped them to overcome—all to point others to Jesus with a message of hope and healing.

Twelve months later, *She Writes for Him: Stories of Resilient Faith* launched on May 12, 2020, featuring best-selling authors, Carol Kent, Tammy Trent, and Dr. Saundra Dalton Smith, and twenty-seven brave women who willingly shared their hard stories of abortion, depression, betrayal, loss, and shame.

Eighteen months later, this second edition you are holding in your hands shouts another testimony of God's goodness as some of my longtime industry and author friends have contributed their redemptive stories. On topics such as suffering, cancer, mental health, addictions, and abuse, this compilation of *She Writes for Him: Stories of Living Hope* continues the legacy God began.

From this series of books, other dreams have been birthed. The podcast *All Things*, based on Romans 8:28, launched in February of 2020, declaring the faithfulness of God in working *all things* together for good.

After the pandemic interrupted our spring and summer conference plans, we hosted our first twenty-one-day *She Writes for Him Bootcamp* and helped forty-plus women go from idea to a manuscript blueprint through ninety-minute interactive virtual workshops, daily writing tips, and multiple coaching sessions.

And then if that weren't enough to keep us busy, God birthed a conference I knew would one day happen but had no idea it would look like this—a virtual conference with three full days and thirty-three-plus publishing professionals and four hundred–plus attendees.

And when the craziness of the pandemic settles, we'll be hosting an in-person intimate writing retreat designed to navigate the author down the path to writing and publishing her story.

From hearing the whisper of God one sunny spring day to watching the *She Writes* vision unfold, it has been an amazing journey of faith. God doesn't mess around when He declares, "Now to him who is able to do far more abundantly than all that we ask or think, according to the power at work within us" (Ephesians 3:20 ESV).

As a reader, you, my friend, are a part of this story and what once was just a little idea. I invite you to join the many women who have found their writing identities through the *She Writes for Him* movement. Don't be surprised if God whispers a dream to your own heart while you are blessed by the healing and hope that radiates from these stories.

To God be the glory!

Athena Dean Holtz, Founder
She Writes for Him
Redemption Press

Part 1

Cancer

Chapter One

The Big C and the Little c

Liz Curtis Higgs

When I first shared my cancer diagnosis on social media, more than one woman commented in all caps, "I HATE CANCER!"

I get it. There's nothing lovable about cancer cells, nothing joyful about malignant tumors, and definitely nothing fun about surgery, chemotherapy, radiation, immunotherapy, and the rest.

But once my unexpected journey began to unfold, I discovered the hope-filled side of going through cancer.

I know. The *what*?!

As I stood with the Lord on the threshold between life and death, I finally grasped how profoundly He is *here for us*. Rather than cancer being a test of our faith, it's a measure of His faithfulness. And, beloved, He passes with flying colors because He is *always* faithful.

My particular brand of cancer was endometrial, so a total hysterectomy came first. I'm fairly certain the long hours of surgery were far harder on my family than on me. When I finally rolled out of recovery at a late hour, we had very little time together before they limped home, exhausted, and I was left alone in a darkened hospital room.

> **Rather than cancer being a test of our faith, it's a measure of His faithfulness.**

I tried to sleep, but couldn't. Tried to sort through my feelings, but couldn't. When I cried out to God in the middle of the night, He was already there, comforting me with His love, just as His Word tells us, "Your love, LORD, reaches to the heavens, your faithfulness to the skies" (Psalm 36:5 NIV). His love and faithfulness also reached into the depths of my soul that night, where fear lurked in the shadows and dread whispered my name.

Cancer, Liz. You have cancer.

Yes, I did. But as a friend shared with me, "Cancer is spelled with a little *c.* Christ is spelled with a big *C.*"

The next morning, my oncologist explained various treatment options, while the Lord gently assured me I could let go of my anxious thoughts and rest in Him. You've no doubt heard this promise: "The peace of God, which transcends all understanding, will guard your hearts and your minds in Christ Jesus" (Philippians 4:7 NIV). To my surprise, I *did* sense His peace in that hospital room, and in a palpable way, like an invisible blanket lightly draped across my shoulders.

A few weeks later, when my hair fell out—all at once, while I was taking a shower—I reminded myself the chemicals were doing exactly what I needed them to do. If my hair follicles were damaged, so were those no-good cancer cells. Friends showered me with silky scarves and knitted caps to cover my shiny bald head, while a greeting card with this verse kept me going: "I remain confident of this: I will see the goodness of the LORD in the land of the living" (Psalm 27:13 NIV).

As my chemotherapy continued, I realized I'd never been more aware of His presence or more in awe of His power. And I'd never felt more compelled to speak His name or sing His praises.

Yes, you lose a few things while you fight the good fight against cancer. My sense of taste went wacko, I had stabbing pains in my hands and feet for a season, and both my big toenails fell off. (Seriously, it's a thing.) But, oh, the joy of knowing my Lord and Savior in new and breathtaking ways—as my comforter, my healer, my deliverer, my friend.

Did my hope ever falter? You bet. If I spent too much time with Dr. Google, I inevitably got discouraged. When my CT scans revealed a new tumor growing in a new place, I wondered if my hope was built on nothing more than wishful thinking. Then I remembered how hope is described in Scripture: "We have this hope as an anchor for the soul, firm and secure" (Hebrews 6:19 NIV). Anchors aren't wishes—anchors are weights, holding us in place.

Though I wouldn't want anyone to go through cancer, I do long for my sisters in Christ to experience firsthand what happens when we accept the reality of our circumstances and not only *trust* God, but also *praise* God for the path He has laid out for us.

Here's one verse that truly says it all. Mind if we unwrap it together?

> Praise be to the God and Father of our Lord Jesus Christ! In his great mercy he has given us new birth into a living hope through the resurrection of Jesus Christ from the dead. (1 Peter 1:3 NIV)

These encouraging words from Peter start where we need to start—where we *must* start—by praising God *with an exclamation point!* We know and love God the Son and God the Holy Spirit, but Peter is pointing us to God the Father, reminding us "how fortunate we are to have him, this Father of our Master Jesus!" (MSG).

If ever we needed to give honor to God, it's in the midst of battling cancer. While our neatly ordered world collapses around us, our heavenly Father remains by our side, immovable and unchangeable. A mighty rock, a fortress, a stronghold, a fortified tower, He deserves to be "gratefully praised and adored" (AMP) because of who He is and because of all He does.

No matter how shaky we might feel emotionally, or how fretful we might be about our physical well-being, God's Word reminds us we are safe, we are secure, and we are altogether His. When the Lord "granted us a new birth" (ISV), we were "spiritually transformed, renewed, and set apart for His purpose" (AMP). Nothing can change that—least of all cancer.

Then comes this beautiful phrase from 1 Peter 1:3, "a living hope" (NIV), which captures the heart of this collection of stories from real women just like you. This is what hope means for us. Not

As my chemotherapy continued, I realized I'd never been more aware of His presence or more in awe of His power.

a faint and fragile hope, but "an ever-living hope" (AMP), filled with "great expectation" (NLT).

When faced with the possibility of leaving this life behind, I was forced to consider what heaven might be like. And guess what? *It's going to be amazing.* This world, much as we cling to it, is not our home. Heaven truly offers *living hope*. It's "an immortal hope" (ISV), a "hope that never dies" (NLV). You and I "have everything to live for, including a future in heaven—and the future starts now!" (MSG).

That future, that living hope, was secured for us by Christ's resurrection. As Peter wrote, "by raising Jesus from death, he has given us new life and a hope that lives on" (CEV). He conquered the grave. He left death in the dust. He showed us the way forward.

At one point during my cancer treatments, I was *so* excited about the thought of meeting the Lord face to face that, when my doctor reported my latest scans showed no evidence of disease, I actually said, "Well, shucks!" (That was a miracle only God could manage, believe me.)

While our neatly ordered world collapses around us, our heavenly Father remains by our side, immovable and unchangeable.

The truth is, what's happening now doesn't matter nearly as much as what's happening next. His plans for us are always good and always purposeful. Whatever the outcome—healing or heaven—God holds out a bright beacon of hope for each one of us.

Cheering you on, beloved.

Living Truth

So do not fear, for I am with you; do not be dismayed, for I am your God. (Isaiah 41:10 NIV)

Living Prayer

Lord Jesus, I confess that sometimes fear still overwhelms me, and a thousand anxious questions crowd my thoughts. Remind me, again and again, that You alone are my living hope, my promise of salvation, my assurance of heaven, and my guarantee of eternal life.

⟶ Living Action

Whether you've been touched by cancer in your own life, or through the life of someone you care deeply about, consider the following:

- What are the best sources you've found for support and encouragement?
- Write out a verse or two from Scripture that bring you comfort and hope.
- What has God taught you through this unexpected journey?

_____

_____

_____

_____

_____

_____

_____

_____

_____

_____

Liz Curtis Higgs has one goal: to help women embrace the grace of God with joy and abandon. She is the author of thirty-seven books, including her nonfiction bestsellers, *Bad Girls of the Bible, The Girl's Still Got It*, and *The Women of Christmas*. Liz has spoken for 1,800 Christian conferences in all fifty states of the US and fifteen foreign countries. Currently she serves as director of the women's ministry team at her church in Louisville, Kentucky. Connect with Liz on Facebook and LizCurtisHiggs.com.

Chapter Two

My Mountain and Valley Experience
Monique Holenko

Unfamiliar territory, a missed exit, and no place to turn around left us with no inkling of the encounter we were going to have. God was going to enlighten me in a firsthand mountain and valley experience. While on holiday in Northern England, my fellow travelers and I found ourselves on an unwelcomed shortcut, Hardknott Pass. This precipitous hill pass from the fourth century, not even wide enough to be named a road, was deemed the most scenic and treacherous pass in all of Britain. It is said nesting within its hills is the home of the loneliest outpost of the Roman Empire.

The view ahead was obscured as the rough asphalt carved its way through a twisted ravine. It was as if it were playing a game of hide and seek with us as it snaked along the mountainside and traversed into the valley for as far as we could see. Abrupt drop-offs, hairpin turns, and steep hill climbs on the thirty-mile route left us novice travelers exhausted, full of trepidation, and apprehension.

Tears streamed down my face as I gave in to panic and worry. My circumstances overcame my capacity for rational thought or ability to recall God's promises. I was a prisoner to a fear I had never known. It was so debilitating I found myself in an irrational state with my head buried in my lap, or was I on the floor?

Just an hour prior and twenty miles away, I had been in a restful state of mind, in the English countryside with its rolling mountains and grassy hills where the sheep roamed freely. I felt as if we were just a moment from heaven as we shared the same space with the clouds.

When we find ourselves in that place, on green hills amid the clouds, life is good. There is a feeling of peace, and recalling God's promises comes so easy. "I lift my eyes to the hills, where does my help come from? My help comes from the Lord, maker of heaven and earth" (Psalm 121:1 NIV).

When my grandmother completed her cancer treatments, elation hung in the air like the clouds over the sheep-scattered mountaintop. But when we were told, "Your father has pancreatic cancer," the joy violently dissipated from the impact of the diagnosis. The very next day we heard, "Your father-in-law has prostate cancer and stage four metastasized lymphoma."

Three terminal cancer diagnoses over the course of just two days, without warning, left me feeling as if my life had veered off a perfectly pleasant road. I felt I was once again in a deep valley with no place to turn around and that I was heading for the ravine.

Cancer can feel like that road in England with all its twists, turns, and obstacles—whether you're the one battling, or it's your wife, husband, brother, sister, daughter, or grandchild. The journey provides no clear instructions or destination. We cry out in fear, "God, where are You?"

When I found myself in that place, God shared with me this truth: In the midst of our despair, if we release the grip on our pain, we can allow the promises of God to carry us to new destinations. God was saying to me, *Open your hands. Drop what you are carrying so you can pick up what I have for you. Peace, love, hope, and joy all are yours, daughter.*

Tears streamed down my face as I gave in to panic and worry. My circumstances overcame my capacity for rational thought or ability to recall God's promises.

As much as we try, it's impossible to pick something up if our hands are full. This is a time when God does not want us to be multitasking, savvy,

I'll-find-a-way-to-handle-it-all women. We *have to* sacrifice something to receive something. Jesus tells us:

> Come to Me, all you who labor and are heavy laden, and I will give you rest. Take My yoke upon you and learn from Me, for I am gentle and lowly in heart, and you will find rest for your souls. For My yoke is easy, and My burden is light. (Matthew 11:28–30 NKJV)

In the midst of our despair, if we release the grip on our pain, we can allow the promises of God to carry us to new destinations.

That revelation is one I wish I had while buried in the back seat of our car that day on the mountain. My grip was so tight around my fear I was blind to receiving anything. I allowed fear to skew my perspective. He was there, and I missed it.

Photos later showed me what I would have seen: snow-topped mountain peaks full of wild flowers and a mountain stream running parallel to the road for the entire journey. It was picture perfect, a Thomas Kinkade painting kind of perfect. If I had lifted my eyes to the hills (literally), I would have seen beauty surrounding me and bringing me the comfort only God can provide when we allow Him.

I am a firm believer that God prepares us and equips us for what is over the next mountain if we walk in faith and truth through the trials of life with Him. Why wouldn't our Heavenly Father want us to be better prepared to fight battles?

Yes, I felt alone when the cancer diagnoses came in. The pain was real. I felt lost and abandoned for a moment. But the Lord reminded me, you can't plow a field looking backward (Luke 9:62 KJV). We can reflect on our past experiences, but we never need to walk that road the same way again.

> Do not yield to fear, for I am always near. Never turn your gaze from me, for I am your faithful God. I will infuse you with my strength and help you in every situation. I will hold you firmly with my victorious right hand. (Isaiah 41:10 TPT)

How enriched are they who find their strength in the Lord; within their hearts are the highways of holiness! Even when their paths wind through the dark valley of tears, they dig deep to find a pleasant pool where others find only pain. He gives to them a brook of blessings filled from the rain of an outpouring. They grow stronger and stronger with every step forward. (Psalm 84:5–7 TPT)

Cancer can attempt to steal our joy and hope, but God offers restoration. Cancer may enslave, but God sets us free. Cancer may destroy, but God makes all things new. Each step in our journey did make us stronger. Our family was blessed with joy, love, hope, and closeness like never before. We celebrated every day the beauty of family in the midst of our trials.

My father was a warrior in this life, but his three-year-battle with pancreatic cancer forced him to lay down his sword. My dear grandmother and my father-in-law both saw their cancer go into remission, still have their swords wielded, and continue fighting onward every day.

Through this experience, I learned living in the present moment and not beyond is all that is required to find joy. Anything beyond the present moment allows our worry to be based on speculation and our minds become a playground for the Enemy's lies. Jesus reminds us in Matthew 6:34 (ESV), "Therefore do not be anxious about tomorrow, for tomorrow will be anxious for itself. Sufficient for the day is its own trouble." God calls us to stand firmly rooted in the truth that we are in the palm of His hand, no matter the circumstances.

I am a firm believer that God prepares us and equips us for what is over the next mountain if we walk in faith and truth through the trials of life with Him.

At the end of our drive along Hardknott Pass, we finally crested the hill and our destination was within view. We collectively breathed a sigh of relief, grateful to have made it through safely. As we approached the crossroad that signaled the end of the road, God reassured us, as He does in all situations, that He has already gone before us. Painted on the pavement were these encouraging words—a tribute to those who journeyed through the challenging course—"Well Done."

～ Living Truth

Do not yield to fear, for I am always near. Never turn your gaze from me, for I am your faithful God. I will infuse you with my strength and help you in every situation. I will hold you with my victorious right hand. (Isaiah 41:10 TPT)

～ Living Prayer

Father God, You are our living hope. Thank You for Your never-ending grace and Your protection over our lives. Help us to have the courage and strength to release from our hands the burdens we have accumulated and pick up the blessings You have prepared for us. Thank You for the trials, Lord. Help us glean from these moments the tools to overcome future battles. Thank You for Your Son who is the only way into the place of perfect peace and rest for our souls.

Cancer may enslave, but God sets us free. Cancer may destroy, but God makes all things new.

~ *Living Action*

- Where in your life could you trust God more?
- Where can you release the grip of control on your situation?
- What Scriptures help you embrace the truth of laying your burdens down at Jesus's feet?

_____

_____

_____

_____

_____

_____

_____

_____

_____

_____

_____

_____

_____

_____

Monique Holenko has a passion for baking and lives out that dream in the bakery she owns with her husband, Alex. She is a worship leader, Bible study teacher, and lover of all things Jesus. Stop by for something sweet for your spirit by visiting her at moniqueholenko.com, Facebook, and Instagram.

Chapter Three

Joy in the Journey
Natasha Lynn Daniels

As I walked with trepidation into my parents' house, I could feel the fear. My husband and I had just received a phone call from my mom minutes earlier. The results from my brother's biopsy came back positive for "testicular germ cell" cancer, and it had spread to his lungs, stomach, hips, liver, and chest.

Born with spina bifida, my brother Izzy had been through many health issues and surgeries his whole life. I was upset with God. *Why, God? Why does he have to suffer yet again? It just isn't fair!* I screamed on the inside, ranting at God about the injustice of it all.

Izzy did not have that attitude. Don't get me wrong, he was afraid, he screamed, he cried, and he had his moments of weakness. However, he never doubted God or questioned why he was struck with cancer. He simply trusted God, held on to his faith, and the Lord became his strength. He believed his battle with cancer would encourage someone. He felt it would all be worth it if one person came to know Christ as their Savior through his suffering.

He also believed this was a test of his new faith in Christ and a temptation from Satan. Nine months before his diagnosis, he had accepted Christ as his Savior

He believed his battle with cancer would encourage someone.

and was baptized, becoming new in Him. He was going to fight this battle in Jesus's name.

I watched my brother worship his way through chemotherapy treatments, sickness, fear, pain, and the loss of all the hair on his head and body. I was inspired by how strong he was through his ordeal. During his treatments he would share Jesus with everyone around him and encourage others. He'd often quote John 16:33 (ESV): "I have said these things to you, that in me you may have peace. In the world you will have tribulation. But take heart; I have overcome the world." My brother truly did have the peace of the Lord and believed God would get him through this tribulation. He knew he would be healed either on this side of heaven or on the other side.

When the chemo made my brother so sick we were not sure he was going to make it, Izzy would tell us, "It's okay if Jesus takes me home."

His credo was modeled on Philippians 1:21 (ESV), "For to me to live is Christ, and to die is gain." His only concern was the grief and sadness our mom would suffer when he was gone. Mom had been his caregiver, he has been her life for thirty-three years, and she didn't know how she would live without him.

After six months of treatments from June to December 2019 and lots of prayer, my brother went into remission. We could not believe he had won the battle over cancer in six months. He continues to go back for scans every three months. Each scan had shown a smaller marker in the lung.

When Izzy had his third scan, the six-month-post scan in July 2020, the report came back positive. His doctor said the marker in the lung was very small and that the CAT scan looked fantastic. Six months after his chemotherapy ended, his hair had grown back, he was eating, he had gained all his weight back, and had no more pain.

As I watched my brother battle cancer with strength from the Lord, peace in his heart, and the joy that lives in him, he became my hero. Watching someone you love suffer through a battle with cancer takes a toll emotionally, spiritually, and physically. Witnessing the miracles of Jesus through His Word reminds me of Paul and Silas and their determination to worship despite the troubles they faced.

Acts 16:25–31 (ESV) reminds us that worshiping and praising God can bring us through the worst of circumstances as Paul and Silas's story relays.

> About midnight Paul and Silas were praying and singing hymns to God, and the prisoners were listening to them, and suddenly there was a great earthquake, so that the foundations of the prison were shaken. And immediately all the doors were opened, and everyone's bonds were unfastened. When the jailer woke and saw that the prison doors were open, he drew his sword and was about to kill himself, supposing that the prisoners had escaped. But Paul cried with a loud voice. "Do not harm yourself, for we are all here." And the jailer called for lights and rushed in and trembling with fear he fell down before Paul and Silas. Then he brought them out and said, "Sirs, what must I do to be saved?" And they said, "Believe in the Lord Jesus, and you will be saved, you and your household."

Paul and Silas were sent to prison, but not once did they doubt God or question Him. They simply worshiped their way through their tribulation. All the prisoners watched how Paul and Silas worshiped because of their faith in God, despite their tribulation. The presence of Jesus was so strong that when the prison doors opened, they didn't leave. Even the jailer wanted to be saved because of what he had witnessed.

Paul is still such an encourager to us today. Hebrews 12:2 (ESV) says, "Looking to Jesus, the founder and perfecter of our faith, who for the joy that was set before him endured the cross, despising the shame, and is seated at the right hand of the throne of God." Jesus set the example by enduring the cross set before Him. He took on our sins and was nailed to the cross so we could have eternal life.

Paul suffered intensely for the Lord and encouraged others in suffering. Paul also exhorts us to keep the faith, hold

As I watched my brother battle cancer with strength from the Lord, peace in his heart, and the joy that lives in him, he became my hero.

`All the prisoners`
`watched how Paul`
`and Silas worshiped`
`because of their faith`
`in God, despite their`
`tribulation.`

on to Jesus, endure whatever cross that is set before us, and to look to Him for our strength.

My brother was and still is an encourager to those who are battling cancer or any illness.

Have you heard the saying, "Happiness is what happens to you, but joy is what happens in you"? I am sure Paul and Silas were not happy they were in jail, just like my brother was not happy he was diagnosed with cancer. But the joy that lived in Paul and Silas is the same joy that gave Izzy the hope he needed to get through the darkness he was battling. He knew he could take heart because Jesus has overcome the world.

Living Truth

Count it all joy, my brothers, when you meet trials of various kinds, for you know that the testing of your faith produces steadfastness. And let steadfastness have its full effect, that you may be perfect and complete, lacking in nothing. (James 1:2–4 ESV)

∾ Living Prayer

Lord, thank You for the joy You give. Let others see the joy that lives in me through my suffering. I know we learn wisdom from the things we endure. Lord, if it's Your will, heal my body from this cancer. When fear and doubt creep in and I am afraid, help me remember You have not given me a spirit of fear. You are fighting my battles. You give peace, not as the world gives, but a peace that surpasses all understanding. Lord, use me to bring You glory, and help me to suffer strong.

∾ Living Action

You can't control what happens to you, but you can control how you respond to the trials of life. We don't sign up for tribulations, but we all face them. God doesn't promise a life without pain, but He does promise He will never leave us alone.

- When you received the diagnosis of cancer, how did you respond?
- Do you have the joy of Jesus in you?
- Do you suffer strong for Him?

> You can't control what happens to you, but you can control how you respond to the trials of life.

Remember, Jesus is the ultimate healer. Worship your way through the storm. James 4:8 (ESV) says, "Draw near to God, and he will draw near to you."

_____

_____

_____

_____

_____

_____

_____

_____

_____

_____

_____

_____

Natasha Lynn Daniels is an author and speaker who has learned to live by faith and find hope during the trials of life. After battling infertility, she was blessed with five children through adoption. She is working on her memoir of God's faithfulness in brokenness and loss that led to the adoption of her children, to be published by Redemption Press. You can find her at natashalynndaniels.com, Facebook: Natasha Lynn Daniels Author and Speaker.

Chapter Four

Cancer Is a Team Sport

T. Elizabeth Renich

In 2005, I was in my second season as the "secretary of defense" at the Washington Redskins, working as administrative assistant to the defensive coaching staff and special teams coordinator. Following months of me not feeling well and ignoring the fact, our team doctor spent the Friday before Memorial Day parading me through a battery of scans, draws, picks, pokes, and prods. He read the test results on the spot. Back in his office, he sat down with me to break the news. The situation was utterly unexpected—for me, not for God—and I was thunderstruck. Ovarian cancer: a disease tagged "a silent killer" with symptoms oftentimes mistaken for other ailments, frequently not detected until too late.

Blindsided, I blurted, "I don't have time for this." Mini-camp was finished and the next batch of off-season practices just a few weeks away. "Do you have any idea how much work I'm in the middle of?"

"This is going to change some things," he predicted, familiar with the demands of both my position and the disease. "We caught it at an early stage, and we're going to do our best to get you through. Are you game?"

He suggested I wait out rush hour at a nearby Italian restaurant. Without consulting a menu, the owner, Ermanno, had a creamy pasta dish brought out from the kitchen. I don't recall what we talked about in the empty private dining room. What I do remember is the compassion I received from this complete stranger.

Ermanno sent me on my way with food enough to last a week. I hadn't any appetite, nor was I eager to go home. For two hours I drove and drove, until I realized I'd be another fifty miles away if I didn't turn my Jeep around. The silence pressed hard as I took a shortcut through a mountain gap. No radio. No music. No phone calls. I couldn't even pray out loud; I had no words.

Behind the distant Alleghenies, God fingerpainted the most stunning sunset across the twilight sky. Breaching the silence, I'm convinced Jesus said, *You are going to have to trust Me. Will you trust Me on this?*

Tears flowed unchecked. "Oh, *Lord*," I cried raggedly, "that's all I can do."

And then I felt His peace as hope folded into the knowledge that He had a purpose.

Having no children of my own, ovarian cancer now confirmed I never would. Nonetheless, throughout my football career, God allowed me to serve as "team mom" for rosters full of players and coaches. I followed His calling to be salt and light off the field.

Everyone at Redskins Park knew I was sick. The news had "broken contain," like a busted play already in action. It was hard to tell if I was executing a defensive strategy or an offensive one. The entire organization—front-office receptionist, coaching staff, coaches' wives, players, scouting department, football operations, and administration—teamed up to orchestrate what I would need before I knew I needed it.

They flew my Momma. in from Minnesota. Dozens wore burgundy-colored silicone wristbands imprinted with the word *BELIEVE* alongside my initials. God was evident in the midst, and He graciously gave me my football family to get through the roughest times. A small huddle of strong believers among the players and staff faithfully showed up to assist and prayed His will would be done

> **Breaching the silence, I'm convinced Jesus said, *You are going to have to trust Me. Will you trust Me on this?***

"to me and through me." They asked God to touch those who knew me and reach those who didn't know me yet.

God was evident in the midst, and He graciously gave me my football family to get through the roughest times.

Caring friends also stepped in with dinners, transportation, housecleaning, and pharmacy runs. One shared Isaiah 43:1–2 (NKJV):

> Fear not, for I have redeemed you; I have called you by your name; you are Mine. When you pass through the waters, I will be with you; and through the rivers, they shall not overflow you. When you walk through the fire, you shall not be burned, nor shall the flame scorch you.

I came out of the operating room thirty pounds lighter than I went in. During the surgical procedures, they drained from my body more than fifteen liters of fluid. God delivered me through those waters—I am His, and He knows my name.

In the waiting room, the surgeon told Momma my tumor was shaped like a small football and remarked, "Good thing she didn't work for the Wizards [basketball team], but too bad she didn't work for the Caps [hockey team]!"

The tumor had been successfully removed, and the prescribed follow-up was chemotherapy. Recovering at home, I gave it all to the Lord again during my twice-daily walk to the mailbox. I prayed if I had to go through this experience and pain it would somehow bolster someone else. God gifted me with a testimony I never asked for, but my hope was in Him.

My first day of chemo was scary. Side effects. Steroids. Anti-nausea pills. Shots. Scans. Losing my hair wasn't anything I looked forward to either. A professor friend organized a group of "wavers" from Marymount. They raised encouraging signs and cheered loudly from the median as we drove past the university campus on the way to Virginia Hospital Center.

My New York Giants–loving oncologist set my chemo schedule according to my weekly in-season routine. Tuesdays were game prep, the "had-to-be-there" days,

God is the only One I know who can bring good out of something that seems so bad.

so he selected Wednesdays for treatments. By lunchtime on Fridays, he said I'd want to be lying down, I may or may not remember Saturdays, but I should be recovered enough to be propped up on Sunday afternoons in time for kickoff. He nailed it.

By mid-November, we'd tackled six treatment protocols, twenty-one days apart. I survived without being burned or scorched too terribly in spite of the harsh chemo drugs, but I did have residual nerve damage in my feet. I continually prayed I would be a good witness to those around me. God is the only One I know who can bring good out of something that seems so bad.

It was a thankful Thanksgiving and a playoff-run Christmas, yet it wasn't until Super Bowl Sunday I set aside my wigs. My hair grew back slowly. Scheduled check-ups came every three months, then six months, then annually.

After those follow-ups, I'd detour past the treatment area, pausing in each room to see if anyone was awake and offer them a smile.

At a Redskins charity event the next season, a breast cancer survivor recognized me and boldly approached. She told me we had been treated in the same oncology practice and relayed how on her first day of chemo she saw me stick my head in her room and smile. When I left, she crossly muttered, "Who is she? Why is she smiling like that?" Her nurse explained I was one of their success stories returning to encourage others going through similar ordeals. That day she determined to fight through her own cancer, hoping to be the next encourager.

In 2010, after a game in Chicago, I found myself riding in the front seat of a squad car with a state trooper on motorcade duty. It was a hurry-up-and-wait scenario until the buses departed the stadium for the airport. Our camaraderie was instant, and it was soon clear why God allowed me to ride with him. His mom was dying of ovarian cancer, but she wasn't forthcoming with answers because she didn't want to worry him. I gave him permission to ask away, and he peppered me with questions I was able to answer because I'd already been through the waters of surgery and the fire of chemo. We kept in touch, later grieving together when we lost our moms within three months of each other. I still pray for him, and I'm grateful God used me to be a part of rekindling his faith.

Four seasons later, God took me out of football, making me His free agent to be a witness far removed from the sidelines. Admittedly, I do not always feel the depth of His presence as keenly as I did while I was sick. But that doesn't mean He isn't with me. Now, as then, choices remain a matter of trust. My hope is in Him, even in the hard and silent waiting, when I can't see what He's doing.

Living Truth

But as for you, you meant evil against me; but God meant it for good, in order to bring it about as it is this day, to save many people alive. (Genesis 50:20 NKJV)

Living Prayer

Lord Jesus, I pray You will draw near to all who read this, to make Yourself known. Steady us with Your gracious love. Let us encourage each other, for our hope is in You. Strengthen our faith to trust You, come what may.

Living Action

A friend recently shared what she learned in a word study. She said trusting, hoping, and waiting on the Lord are like the binding of a threefold cord, one not quickly or easily broken.

My hope is in Him, even in the hard and silent waiting, when I can't see what He's doing.

- Have you experienced that His strength is made perfect in your weakness?
- How have you learned God is trustworthy?
- Do you trust His timing, and that He will not waste anything or any situation?
- When was the last time you turned around to see how the puzzle pieces came together and gave God the glory?

_____

_____

_____

_____

_____

_____

_____

_____

_____

_____

Shadowcreek Chronicles author T. Elizabeth Renich worked for two NFL teams and visited all fifty United States before her fiftieth birthday. She hunts historical markers and shares hope as an ovarian cancer survivor. Addicted to Shutterfly.com, her love of photography is evident in photo books documenting research trips and life. You can find her at t.elizabeth .renich.net and Facebook.com/telizabethshadowcreekbooks.

Chapter Five

Hope When You've Been Given a Cancer Diagnosis
Dr. Michelle Bengtson

I'm quite certain I won't ever forget the day I was diagnosed with cancer.

About a week earlier, I had shared what I thought was a very mild concern with my doctor. She then determined a biopsy was in order.

"A biopsy? Oh, I hardly think all that is necessary," I implored.

Still she insisted.

"Okay—do as you like, but I don't think we need to make that big of a fuss over it. It's more of an annoyance than anything."

Honestly, I put it behind me and didn't consider it again until my husband and I were in the car, headed to his appointment with his oncologist. My cell phone rang in my lap, startling me. I looked at the caller ID, which displayed the name of my doctor's office in big capital letters. I assumed they were just calling to remind me of my follow-up appointment.

"Hello," I answered cheerfully.

"Dr. Bengtson?"

"Yes, this is she."

> We sat waiting to see his doctor, holding hands and drawing strength from each other.

She shared her identity and asked if it was a convenient time to talk. After I added my consent, she proceeded. "I'm sorry to have to tell you this, but you have cancer."

I sat stunned for what felt like minutes, but could only have been a second or two before responding, "Excuse me? What did you say?"

She repeated the words no one ever expects or wants to hear, "I'm sorry, but you have cancer. We will need to schedule surgery."

This couldn't be. We were on our way to my husband's oncologist to learn of his health status after his three-time war on cancer.

Thoughts raced through my head. *I wouldn't be surprised if we get a bad report from my husband's doctor, but me? I'm healthy. I just went in because it was a nuisance. This can't be. I have things to do. Holidays to prepare for. How can they be sure?*

My thoughts were abruptly brought to a halt when she interrupted, "Could we schedule that now?"

I was in such a state of shock that I couldn't think, much less navigate a phone and a calendar at the same time. "Um, I'll have to call you back . . ."

After we hung up, my husband looked at me. "Everything okay?"

In a voice that sounded foreign to my own ears, I relayed what I had just been told. He had questions I couldn't answer. I had even more questions. We would have to just sit with them and make it through his appointment.

We sat waiting to see his doctor, holding hands and drawing strength from each other. At one point, I realized I had been holding my breath and had to intentionally remind myself to breathe.

As we sat in silence, neither one of us saying a word, knowing the other's thoughts. The phone conversation with the doctor replayed over and over in my mind. *Where do we go from here?* I wondered.

It was then I realized I had a choice. I could slip down that slippery slope into worry, fear, and anxiety. I could be overwhelmed, and expect catastrophe, or I could claim His peace. I had just turned in my manuscript to my publisher for my next book, *Breaking Anxiety's Grip: How to Reclaim the Peace God Promises* about exchanging our worries, fears, and anxieties for God's peace. It appeared the Enemy was testing me to see if I believed my message. But I had written the blueprint for how to manage worry, fear, and anxiety. Now I would choose to live it.

I chose to stand firm on these truths:

1. Even though I was stunned, this did not take God by surprise (Jeremiah 29:11).
2. God is still on His throne, and He is still in the miracle-making business (Psalm 47:8).
3. I will not die but live, and proclaim what the Lord has done (Psalm 118:17).
4. Jesus warned we would have trials in this life, but He has overcome them all (John 16:33).
5. When I am weak, He is strong (2 Corinthians 12:10).
6. No weapon formed against me shall prosper, not even cancer (Isaiah 54:17).
7. By His stripes I am healed (Isaiah 53:5).
8. God has always been faithful before, and I have no reason to doubt Him now (Deuteronomy 7:9).
9. The Lord is close to the brokenhearted and saves the crushed in spirit (Psalm 34:18).
10. God's plans are to prosper me and not to harm me, and they include a future and a hope (Jeremiah 29:11).
11. He who began a good work in me will see it through to completion (Philippians 1:6).
12. I do not need to be afraid, because He will be with me wherever I go (Joshua 1:9).
13. Greater is He who is in me than he who is in the world (1 John 4:4).
14. God will fight this battle for me, if I will only be still (Exodus 14:14).
15. God will use even this cancer diagnosis for good and for His glory (Romans 8:28).
16. God has not given me the spirit of fear, but of power, love, and a sound mind (2 Timothy 1:7).

17. God will be my comforter through this, so I can then comfort others with the comfort He has given me (2 Corinthians 1:3–4).
18. Ultimately, my hope comes from God. Because of Him, hope prevails (Psalm 62:5).

As I thought through these various truths, I realized the importance of knowing what we believe before a crisis hits, so when it does our core beliefs will sustain us during the difficult times. Within a minute, I had to decide whether or not I was going to believe all the lies swirling around in my head, and cave to worry, fear, and anxiety, or I was going to find comfort in my long-standing beliefs based on the truths of God's Word.

The cancer journey has not been an easy one. Doctors make their best predictions, but only God knows the number of our days. Having been not just a cancer patient, but a caregiver for a three-time cancer surviving husband and a mother with lung cancer—and the chief neuropsychologist for pediatric hematology/oncology patients—I've learned that each day is a gift. While the days throughout the cancer journey can have their ups and downs, the one truth I hold on to is that as long as God remains on His throne, every day is a good day for a good day!

I continue to stand on these truths and rest in the knowledge that God is in control, and that I am safe in the shelter of His wings.

Will you cling to His truths today?

I realized the
importance of knowing
what we believe before
a crisis hits, so when
it does our core beliefs
will sustain us during
the difficult times.

～ Living Truth

I would have despaired unless I had believed that I would see the goodness of the LORD in the land of the living. (Psalm 27:13 NASB)

～ Living Prayer

Father, You know our human reaction to receiving devastating diagnoses and prognoses from the medical profession, yet Your Word says You are our healer. Help us to put our trust in You, knowing You've ordained each day we are granted breath and life. Help us to live each day to the fullest for You and Your kingdom, while trusting You to give us strength for each new day and each new task You call us to. Thank You that You remain our comforter, our provider, and the lifter of our heads in the painful trials of life.

∽ Living Action

- Prayerfully consider some of the lies you've been tempted to believe during the difficulties of life.
- Ask the Holy Spirit to reveal scriptural truth to refute and combat those lies.
- Memorize those Scriptures.

_____

_____

_____

_____

_____

_____

_____

_____

_____

_____

_____

_____

Dr. Michelle Bengtson is a cancer survivor and wife to a three-time cancer survivor. She is a clinical neuropsychologist, an international speaker, and a national and international media resource on mental health. She has authored three best-selling, award-winning books. She hosts Your Hope-Filled Perspective podcast and has many resources at DrMichelleB.com.

Chapter Six

"I'm Sorry—It's Cancer"

Debbie Alsdorf

Through waves, and clouds, and storms, He gently clears the way.
—L. B. Cowman, *Streams in the Desert*

It was the beginning of June 2013, and like many other months, I had picked a Scripture to sit with as I started each day. That June would be forever marked by starting my mornings with coffee and Psalm 103.

"Praise the Lord, my soul, and forget not all his benefits—who forgives all your sins and heals all your diseases, who redeems your life from the pit and crowns you with love and compassion" (Psalm 103:2–4 NIV).

Psalm 103 speaks of the benefits of a life lived to God and goes on to describe the nature of God as compassionate, gracious, and abounding in love. In the daily reading of the Psalm there was one particular phrase that struck a chord with me: "forget not all his benefits." Or, more succinctly, "forget not"! It became clear that God was reminding me to pay attention to who He is and how He loves me.

June was also the month for my routine medical exams. As usual, I went for my yearly mammogram without a symptom, lump, or complaint. I never worried about the screenings because there wasn't a history of breast cancer in my family. Imagine my surprise when the call came that a suspicious finding required a biopsy—and the shock a few weeks later when the doctor called to tell me the results.

There is no way to sugar coat the word cancer. Though we often do when it is someone else's diagnosis, but when it's our body and our news, it's a bit surreal. The shock of that word and the immediate dread is so strong that we remember that moment.

It was midmorning and my newly retired husband and I were just about to leave to go watch our infant grandson Easton. I grabbed the phone and silently listened as the oncology radiologist spoke that *C* word over me and then outlined my next steps. It felt like a dream—or nightmare. As she talked and my husband's face drained of all color, I took quick notes. The entire call I boldly scribbled in the margins of my notepad, "Forget Not! Forget Not! Forget Not!" It became obvious to me there was no coincidence that I was sitting in Psalm 103 each day—God was going before me, preparing the way. He was calling me to remember His goodness, even in a cancer diagnosis.

Everything began to move quickly; within twenty-four hours I had a meeting with the breast cancer nurse and was set up to meet with my oncology team, surgeon, and radiologist. The surgery would take place in a week, followed by six weeks, or thirty treatments of radiation. This would be followed by five years on an estrogen-blocking cancer drug, filled with the promise of side effects. My calendar was turned upside down, my speaking engagements doled out to other speaker friends, and my plans for the next few months suspended with no new plans in sight. It was clear, I would have to walk through the fire in order to be healed.

After the radiation treatments, I began the drug that made my body hurt as if I were ninety. Just walking hurt and every move amplified pain. Clearly, I was having all the side effects. Between horrid hot flashes and tears, the discouragement of it all was starting to get to me. I hadn't slept much, pain from radiation kept me up tossing, turning, and burning. As I applied lotions and potions to my body, I hardly recognized one part of me—the

> God was going before me, preparing the way. He was calling me to remember His goodness, even in a cancer diagnosis.

part that nursed babies and satisfied my husband. I wondered endlessly during the night how it would heal, because I was told it would. I wondered in the quietness of the night if the cancer would return, because I know it can.

> I committed myself to worship in the middle of the pain and days of discouragement.

And as I wondered and silently cried, I turned my eyes upon something greater. A door of hope began to open in my mind. That hope was not based on things resolving like I want them to; it was much greater than that. The hope was based on the plan and goodness of God in the middle of this current trouble.

I committed myself to worship in the middle of the pain and days of discouragement.

At first it was hard. I sat at my piano and played a chord progression as I read in tears the Psalms. Then I began singing "10,000 Reasons" by Matt Redmon. Barely mumbling the lyrics, I began to worship and bless the Lord. Initially the words were just half utterances through tears. I mean, this girl was discouraged—life had been hitting hard. Right after radiation was finished, my lower leg was cast for a tendon tear. One more thing. *Really? Really, Lord?*

But as I began to rise above and venture into praise, through tears, something happened.

It was like a miracle. My own personal miracle. Thanking God works. Focusing on Him works. This is abundance, that I have a personal relationship with God. I hesitated telling anyone because I didn't want to exclaim about one day of joy. But after over three weeks of immense joy, I began to realize I needed to share the power of praise with those I knew and loved. And, when I was tempted to crawl back into the den of discouragement, I'd lift my hands, my head, my heart, and I begin to sing or praise or recite the truth, of God's Word.

Call me a fanatic of faith, or recognize I am a broken woman like the rest of the world and pay attention to what I am saying. God paves a way for us through His Word. His Word is truth, and truth sets us free.

"Rejoice always; pray continually, give thanks in all circumstances; for this is God's will for you in Christ Jesus" (1 Thessalonians 5:16–18 NIV).

Thanking God works.
Focusing on Him works.

The word *will* here denotes "delight or pleasure." It is God's delight and pleasure that we remain joyful, connected to Him in prayer and grateful to Him in thanks. His pleasure!

If you are discouraged, please don't discount this. Give it a try, even through your tears. God loves you so much. Could it be that this discouraging moment will become a memory someday of a time when you began drawing closer to the Father's heart, in spite of the circumstances? Could it be that God really can deposit joy into our souls? I believe all things are possible with God!

I am currently a seven-year breast cancer survivor. But at year six, when I thought it couldn't happen again, I got the call saying I needed a biopsy. Something looked suspicious. Had the cancer returned? Two surgical biopsies later, and after two weeks of waiting for results, the call came that it was a benign finding.

But during those two weeks I had peace. In fact, I had tremendous peace. Because you see, over this cancer journey I had adopted my own acronym for joy—Jesus Over You. And I believe it with all my heart. Jesus is over me, He is over you, and because of this we can have hope.

Please don't misunderstand; I am not flippant about cancer. Last year I lost two dear friends who were like family to cancer. They were much younger than me. Months later my own husband was diagnosed with melanoma. Cancer has hit close to home, and yet, I confess and believe that Jesus is over me. I remember who He is and how He loves—and I have peace.

Where are you today? Do you need to turn back the page to believe more fully again? Have you faced the *C* word or have a loved one who has? He knows. And I know this too: He is waiting, bidding you and me to come close, to trust more, to experience the breath of heaven in the heat of earth's battle.

 *Living Truth*

The Lord is my shepherd, I lack nothing. (Psalm 23:1 NIV)

So do not fear, for I am with you. Do not be dismayed, for I am your God. I will strengthen you and help you. I will uphold you with my righteous right hand. (Isaiah 41:10 NIV)

~ *Living Prayer*

Lord Jesus, I come to You today—again. Cancer has felt like a vast army coming against me. And the attack has not been just physical but also mental and emotional. I need You. I ask for fresh faith and renewed hope during this season and in every follow-up season that I must live with for the rest of my life. I ask You to transform any area of unbelief in my heart as I seek to believe in Your healing power through all of the seasons of my life. I pray for hope—a heavenly outlook that produces endurance in me. I praise You for loving me, caring for me, and shepherding me. Most importantly I thank You that You heal all my diseases and crown me with Your love and compassion. For Your goodness, I am most grateful.

~ *Living Action*

- Today is a good day to begin looking up or continuing to look up. Make it a commitment just like you would any other action on your calendar. Today is a day to "forget not." Remember who God is and how He loves you.
- Watch your words of discouragement during this season. Though sharing our hearts with those close to us is to be encouraged, a constant dripping of negative talk will only bring us down. Instead of complaining, try turning that around to "Thank You, Lord. Though this is hard, You are with me."

He is waiting, bidding you and me to come close, to trust more, to experience the breath of heaven in the heat of earth's battle.

- Resist the urge to bury yourself in medical journals, choosing to fill your mind with the beauty of what is good and lovely. You can do this through choosing good things to read and watch during this time. If you aren't feeling well, invite a friend to come hang out with you on the couch watching romantic comedies or anything that might bring laughter to your soul.
- Try "sitting" in Scripture, maybe on one chapter, passage, or psalm at a time. Read it quietly and out loud. Memorize the parts that fill your heart with hope.
- Don't waste today. Cancer or not, none of us know how many days we have. Continue to be kind, to pray, and to ask for help when needed—but don't waste this day. Look for a sparkle of hope everywhere you go.

_____

_____

_____

_____

_____

_____

_____

_____

_____

Debbie Alsdorf's mission is to lead women to the heart of God's love through the truth of His Word. She is an international speaker, the author of twelve books, and has been featured on the Aspire Women's Events Tour. After a lifetime in California, Debbie and her husband Ray now make their home in Arizona. They have raised a blended family of four children and have nine grandlittles who call her Grammy. Visit her at debbiealsdorf.com.

Part 2

Addiction

Chapter Seven

Set Free to Love
Pam Farrel

I grew up in a home full of chaos due to the abusive behaviors induced by the alcohol addiction of my dad. To be fair, his father was the town drunk, and his granddad also struggled with the bottle. Beer and hard liquor are like the sap running through my family tree. The worst night in my relationship with my drinking dad was when I was a freshman in college. Dad had been drinking all day and all night (which he did daily), and my sweet mom was trying in futility to calm his rage.

About midnight things had calmed. This chaos happened daily, so Mom encouraged us to go to bed. Mom's 3:00 a.m. scream of "Help me! Help me!" shocked us awake. We ran through the pitch-black house, thinking Dad's anger had escalated, and we needed to rescue Mom. My brother burst through the garage door, and before us was my dad trying to hang himself from the rafters of the garage. My brother pulled my dad down, we all dragged him into the house, and we tackled him onto the sofa. As we knelt on his chest, I took the noose off his neck. Remembering the Bible story of crazy King Saul and David, the harp player, I thought, *Music! We need church music!* So as we knelt on our agitated, out-of-control dad for hours, we sang "Amazing Grace" to save the life of my dad.

Apart from a miracle intervention of God, studies say we tend to repeat these harmful and dysfunctional family patterns. In our books, *Men Are Like Waffles, Women Are Like Spaghetti* and *7 Simple Skills for Every Woman*, we share the full story of redemption, reconciliation, and restoration, including six steps of forgiveness to help give God control of our hearts and lives in a way that heals and brings hope. Regardless of how we were treated in our homes of origin, or previous relationships, we can decide to love and live differently. When we love like Jesus, we become better, freer, more loving people, and we give others, even the broken, the addict, and the toxic the hope of learning to live and love in freedom as well.

Broken to Blessing

God also gives us some specific commands to bless and be a blessing so we can live freely:

> Bless those who curse you, pray for those who mistreat you. (Luke 6:28 NIV)

> Bless those who persecute you; bless and do not curse . . . Live in harmony with one another. . . . If it is possible, as far as it depends on you, live at peace with everyone. Do not take revenge, my dear friends, but leave room for God's wrath, for it is written: "It is mine to avenge; I will repay," says the Lord. On the contrary: "If your enemy is hungry, feed him; if he is thirsty, give him something to drink. In doing this, you will heap burning coals on his head." Do not be overcome by evil, but overcome evil with good (Romans 12:14–21 NIV).

Beer and hard liquor
are like the sap
running through my
family tree.

As a young mom, when I read these verses in a quiet time with God, I knew even though I had already forgiven my dad for every hurt and pain I could remember, God was calling me to be a blessing and to write a blessing. I wanted to share the love of God with my dad

Regardless of how we were treated in our homes of origin, or previous relationships, we can decide to love and live differently.

and open the door of grace and mercy for him, should he become ready to walk through into the loving arms of the God who could finally give peace to his soul.

I prayed, "God, I am having a hard time recalling a happy memory or moment on which to write this blessing. If You help me remember one, I will write a blessing and give it to Dad for Christmas." That night as I dreamed, I remembered a precious day when I was a very young girl. The next morning, I got up early and wrote the blessing. I knew I had to give the blessing expecting nothing in return, and I should be prepared for a negative response. I was doing this "unto Jesus" (1 Corinthians 10:31). On Christmas Day, I called Dad aside so it was just he and I, then read this blessing to my father:

Our Golden Treasure

It was a sunny Saturday morning. Excited children piled out of cars, baskets in hand. It was the day before Easter, the day of our small town's big egg hunt. I was nervous and excited, as were all the other preschoolers. I held tight to my dad's hand. The whistle blew, and the race to find the prized golden egg was on! I picked up a pink egg and then a green one, and I placed them gently in my basket. But what I really wanted was that golden egg. The hunt seemed as though it lasted a lifetime. It seemed that no one could find the golden egg.

Dad said, "Come here, honey."

He bent down and whispered into my ear and pointed at the ground. I looked down at a disgusting sight—an egg smashed and broken from being trampled upon by tiny feet.

"But it's broken!" I said to my dad.

"What color is it, Charlie?"

I shrugged my shoulders.

"Look close. What color do you see?"

I tried hard to find a piece of shell big enough to discern its color. I picked up a small fragment and whispered, "It's gold! Daddy, it's gold!" But how was I supposed to get it over to the judges?

"Pick it up. Moms and dads can't touch the prized egg. You have to carry it."

"Ick! It's too yucky, Daddy! I can't."

"If you want the prize, you have to pick it up. But I will help you carry it."

We bent down, and I scooped up as much of the egg remnant as my tiny hands could carry. It felt awful. Dad slid his hand under mine, and together we carried our broken treasure to the judges. I was awarded a huge basket brimming with Easter goodies. Dad was proud of me, and I was proud of him.

In the years since, I have often thought of that day. It is a picture of our father-daughter relationship. My dad is a lot like that broken golden egg. He has often felt inadequate to be all that he wanted to be as a dad. His heart is like that egg—full of prize-winning potential but cracked by the heartache of broken dreams. Dad has a heart of gold, but it often goes unseen by those around him. Words fail him. Sometimes his actions fall short of the feelings he'd like to express. But I've always held on to a piece of that prizewinning potential, just like I held on to that small piece of golden shell. I've held on to the golden moments that Dad and I have shared. Like that day in the park, when I was proud of him, and he was proud of me. And when times are hard, I sometimes hear that whisper, "If you want the prize, you have to pick it up."

So I gather up the pieces of life and carry what life requires me to carry.

No, Dad is not perfect, but neither am I. So I hold tight to that less-than-perfect treasure because all that has happened—the good and the bad—God has used to make me the woman I've wanted to be. I have become a woman who can look at a bad situation, find the gold in it, and go on.

I'm a prizewinner in my daddy's eyes, and his love is a golden treasure to me.[1]

As I handed him the framed blessing, he began to weep. A man who had never read any of my writing (that I knew of), a man who had never heard any of my speeches, complimented me, and he blessed me back:

"Charlie, thank you for using your fine words to say such nice things about this good ol' bad ol' boy. If you think sharing our story might help other folks, you just share it then, Charlie girl." And he gave me a rare hug and wiped away his tears. I sensed he felt free from the load of guilt and shame he had been carrying.

Not many weeks later, I couldn't get Dad on the phone, so I called the sheriff's department of his community and asked them to do a drive-by to check on him. They had gone by on other occasions because he had been suicidal, and they also knew he had a heart condition. This night however, about midnight, I got the call that my father had passed from this life.

I was the executor of the will and had his house key, so immediately I met my siblings at his home. When I walked in, I could tell where he had spent his last hours. There at his desk was the stack of Christian books and videos each of the family members had given him. The resources had been read, dog-eared, and watched. Sitting on top of the pile was a *Steps to Peace with God* booklet. The booklet was opened to the prayer of surrender. Pulled forward, as if he had been reading it moments before he entered

> I have become a woman who can look at a bad situation, find the gold in it, and go on.

I knew I had done everything I could to show Dad the love of God.

eternity, was the "Our Golden Treasure" blessing I had written him.

When I read the tribute one last time to him as I placed his ashes in the cold Kansas ground that winter, there was a sense of peace and freedom. I knew I had done everything I could to show Dad the love of God, and I believe he finally gave in to our gracious God and was ushered into heavenly peace.

Living Truth

And God is able to bless you abundantly, so that in all things at all times, having all that you need, you will abound in every good work. (2 Corinthians 9:8 NIV).

Living Prayer

Lord, You promise a blessing to me, that I will be given all I need for every good work. I need wisdom to know the next steps in seeing You heal my heart so I can become a heart healer too. Please bless me so I in turn can be a blessing to others. Please pour Your love into me so I can love others with Your love.

~ *Living Action*

Who in your world needs to be loved with Christ's love? Ask God how He wants you to express love and blessing to another—then do it.

- Is God calling you to forgive someone who has offended you? It will free you to bless someone who may have been hurtful, unhealthy, or toxic.
- Is there someone God wants you to write a note to, create a gift for, or give goodness toward?
- Find a way to bless someone who needs to be freed from the shame, guilt, or brokenness caused by their past unwise choices.

_____

_____

_____

_____

_____

_____

_____

_____

Pam Farrel is a relationship specialist, co-director with her husband Bill of Love-Wise.com, and the author of forty-plus books, including her newest, *7 Simple Skills for Every Woman: Success in Keeping Everything Together*, which includes how to forgive, set healthy boundaries to salvage or protect a relationship, and write a tribute or blessing to your own hard-to-love person. Visit her at Love-Wise.com/simpleskills.php.

Chapter Eight

Three Big Truths
Carol A. Larson

I have to stop doing this, I told myself for the millionth time. I wasn't going to do this again. I was chained to the computer screen, drinking in the degrading pictures as if I were parched. My mind was screaming at me to stop looking, telling me, *I'm supposed to be a good Christian woman.* But my body was rebelling, demanding to feel pleasure, all while I scolded myself.

For ten years I continued to numb the pain and shame that reminded me I was imperfect and unable to please others. I tried to keep my "do good" Christian mask on. I knew I was fooling everyone, including myself, by not measuring up to what I thought it meant to be a good Christian.

Viewing pornography became a compulsive addiction I ran to daily. Excuses I used included emotional disappointments, challenging projects, loneliness, and celebrations of success. I could not wait to get home after work, anticipating viewing my favorite websites and knowing a pleasurable rush was right around the corner. Even knowing I would feel more pain and shame afterward no longer deterred me. The rebel within me emerged and vowed to never back down again.

I Can't

I realized too late I was being sucked deeper and deeper into the quicksand of addiction. The pornography pulled me in deeper each time I resisted.

I pleaded with God to take my craving away. I white-knuckled a couple of days, determined to quit. I stopped sinking in the quicksand, but I couldn't get out either. I always returned after a hard day at work or a difficult conversation with someone, and again I sank deeper.

One day in November 2003, I realized I wanted more than what I was getting from my computer screen. I wanted to step out into the real world to get real sex and the intimacy I desperately craved. Immediately, fear welled up inside me. I was not a risk-taker, or so I thought, yet the rebel in me wanted more. I feared my "good Christian woman" reputation was nearing destruction. I knew I would soon disappear further into the quicksand. The rebel was not convinced getting out of this quagmire was worth it. I knew this insanity needed to stop, yet I continued wrestling against the images in my mind. Feelings of shame wrapped around me like a wet wool blanket. I knew the dangers of leaving the "safety" of my home to find action out there would only take me under.

Paul described the very thoughts I was having. "I do not understand what I do. For what I want to do I do not do, but what I hate I do" (Romans 7:15 NIV).

He further lamented: "For I know that good itself does not dwell in me, that is, in my sinful nature. For I have the desire to do what is good, but I cannot carry it out. For I do not do the good I want to do, but the evil I do not want to do—this I keep on doing. Now if I do what I do not want to do, it is no longer I who do it, but it is sin living in me that does it" (Romans 7:18–20 NIV). Paul moved past his denial and concluded: "What a wretched man I am! Who will rescue me from this body that is subject to death?" (Romans 7:24 NIV).

I tried to keep my "do good" Christian mask on. I knew I was fooling everyone, including myself.

I, too, realized my denial of my dependency on pornography was only getting me into a hopeless place. Telling myself I could get out of this was futile.

I admitted I was powerless over my sin nature (my flesh), and that the rebel inside me was in control. It was impossible to be a good Christian woman on my own.

It was impossible to be a good Christian woman on my own.

The porn and finding sex for real offered a deceptive way out of this quicksand. I felt like I was reaching for a loaded shotgun to grab and escape the quicksand, knowing the chance to grab that gun would only lead to destruction and death.

I knew I needed help. I was helpless and without hope. I vowed to tell someone of my problem and get help, no matter how embarrassed I would be. I chose a dear trusted friend to tell my secret to, who happened to be a counselor.

Paul also cried out to the Lord in a moment of desperation. He told the Corinthians about the time he pleaded with the Lord to remove his problem.

"Therefore, in order to keep me from becoming conceited, I was given a thorn in my flesh, a messenger of Satan, to torment me. Three times I pleaded with the Lord to take it away from me" (2 Corinthians 12:7–8 NIV).

Paul received this response from Jesus. "But he said to me, 'My grace is sufficient for you, for my power is made perfect in weakness'" (2 Corinthians 12:9 NIV).

I first had to get past my own denial of having power over my addiction. The truth is I lacked the power to stop giving into the cravings and desires of my flesh. *I can't* became my first big truth.

Jesus Can

As I meditated on Jesus's words to Paul, I realized I needed to put my trust in Jesus. He promised His grace is enough. This means adequate, always enough, never running out. And even more important, Jesus's power is perfect in my weakness. It comes down to my letting go of the need to be in control of my life. I wasn't doing a very good job anyway, allowing my rebel to be in charge. Jesus does have the power to change my life. My second big truth became *Jesus can.*

I Will Let Him

Paul and I next encountered the need to let go of being in control and allowing Jesus to give us His grace and power. Paul explained to both the Corinthians and the Romans how he did this.

"Therefore I will boast all the more gladly about my weaknesses, so that Christ's power may rest on me. That is why, for Christ's sake, I delight in weaknesses, in insults, in hardships, in persecutions, in difficulties. For *when I am weak, then I am strong*" (2 Corinthians 12:9–10 NIV, emphasis mine).

"Thanks be to God, who delivers me through Jesus Christ our Lord! . . . Therefore, there is now no condemnation for those who are in Christ Jesus, because through Christ Jesus the law of the Spirit who gives life has set you free from the law of sin and death" (Romans 7:25; 8:1–2 NIV). Jesus Christ has the power to save us and change us. He is the one who will manage our lives the best. It is utterly amazing and beyond comprehension how Jesus gives His grace so freely. Jesus exchanges our sins for His righteousness. Thus we are righteous in God's eyes as we ask for forgiveness and receive His righteousness. We are loved, seen as saints, and assured of life forever with Him. Jesus defeated sin, death, and Satan's power.

My third truth is *I will let Him.* In other words, we willingly surrender to Jesus's grace and power, allowing Him to oversee our life and our will.

Today, I have over thirteen years of sobriety, all because Jesus has redeemed, renewed, and restored me through the help of counselors, accountability partners who knew my secrets, much prayer, and humbly surrendering to God's will. I am healed because I chose to let God be in control, receiving His grace, mercy, forgiveness, and righteousness, instead of continuing to allow my rebellious flesh to have her way.

The truth is I lacked the power to stop giving into the cravings and desires of my flesh.

May we all consider choosing to receive all He is offering us. Paul asked in 1 Corinthians 4:7 (NIV), "What do you have that you did not receive?"

God gave His gift of grace to us through His Son, Jesus. It is our choice to receive or reject all God gives us. His grace includes salvation, forgiveness, power, and righteousness. Have you received all God has given you?

✒ *Living Truth*

God made him [Jesus] who had no sin to be sin for us, so that in him we might become the righteousness of God. (2 Corinthians 5:21 NIV)

✒ *Living Prayer*

Lord Jesus, I know I have tried so hard to do things my own way and failed time and time again. Please forgive me for my selfishness. I acknowledge Your grace is enough for me. I choose to let go of my sins and to receive Your righteousness. Help me find someone to share my secret with. Thank You.

I am healed because I chose to let God be in control.

➤ *Living Action*

- **Truth 1:** *I can't.* When have you found yourself trying to stop doing something you did not want to do, yet did it anyway? Acknowledge you are powerless.
- **Truth 2:** *Jesus can.* Jesus has the power to help you change and bring sanity to your life once again. Ask for help. Who is a safe person you can reach out to and tell your secret? There is freedom in bringing your secret out into the light.
- **Truth 3:** *I will let Him.* What has Jesus already given to you that you have not yet received? Let go of your sins and receive Jesus's righteousness.

_____

_____

_____

_____

_____

_____

_____

_____

_____

_____

Carol A. Larson, MSEd, MA, is a private-practice mental health counselor, teacher, international speaker, Bible study leader, and writer. She enjoys music, playing piano, reading, photography, traveling to national parks, and spoiling her nieces, nephews, and cat. Visit her blog at carolalarson.com and email her at carollarsonflc@gmail.com.

Chapter Nine

Exposing Family Secrets
Paula Jauch

This past fall I received another Facebook notification that a young family member had passed away from an overdose. As heavy as this news sounds, this is pretty much the normal in my family. Sometimes I feel numb to it, because I am not even sure how to respond anymore. I wish I could say this wasn't a true story, but it is.

I know this is heavy stuff to write about, but I also know how important it is to let others know they are not alone. After sharing my story through radio or speaking, I encounter numerous people who are hurting due to a loved one using drugs or alcohol or unhealed trauma in their life. I could share many stories about how addiction has affected my life—the incarceration, suicide, overdoses, homelessness, and much more, but instead I want to help you understand there is hope for your situation.

My Story

The nagging voices in my head were loud. I could no longer fight the torment I was feeling. At age twenty-one I was renting a house in Las Vegas with

The nagging voices in my head were loud. I could no longer fight the torment I was feeling.

the help of a government program. My three children were between the ages of six months and six years old. This was a time that they needed their mommy, but the feeling I had to relieve myself of the pain was greater than their needs at the time. You may not understand this, but this is a true feeling that comes with suicidal thoughts.

I remember walking into my bedroom that day, opening the door of my closet, and shutting myself in. I sat on the floor processing how I could stop the dark feelings. I was a cutter, so I thought, *Maybe if I cut a little deeper that will stop the pain.*

As I sat there on the floor contemplating suicide, out of nowhere my thoughts shifted, and I started to see all the people over the years who told me God loves me and has a plan for my life. As I started to wrestle with these thoughts, I began to weep. My six-year-old opened the door and looked at me. He said, "I hate you, Mommy. All you do is cry!" He slammed the door and walked away. Then I heard the voice of an old coworker, *Jesus loves you, and He wants to heal your heart.* When she spoke these words to me, I really didn't care what she had to say. It was confusing for me to understand, and she was way too happy for me to even try to receive what she was saying.

But at that moment in the closet, I felt a nudge telling me, *Don't give up.* In the midst of my hopelessness, I opened my mouth and cried out to God, "If You are real, I *need* to know You now!" It was a cry for help.

As I lay there on the closet floor, a peace penetrated my heart. That peace was something I had never experienced before, and I wanted to tell someone who would understand what was going on. Then I thought of my neighbor, the annoying guy who kept putting Jesus pamphlets on my car before I went to work. I placed my babies on the couch and looked each one in the face. I told them, "Mommy will be right back." With confidence in my voice I said, "Your mommy is never going to be the same." I just knew something in my heart had changed. I ran across the street to my neighbor's house and told him what happened. With joy on his face, he came over to my house and laid his hand on my shoulder and started to pray with me.

Healing the Broken Pieces

I grew up in abuse and neglect, surrounded by addiction from the time I was born. With a father who was incarcerated and a mother absent because of addiction, I wasn't even aware that my needs weren't being met as a child.

Pregnant at fifteen years old, I was initiated into a Hispanic gang because I longed to be accepted into a family. School was a struggle; I was placed in special education classes and various behavioral programs until I was kicked out of school and sent to an alternative education program.

As an adult woman these things still plagued me as I tried to get a job and found myself only reading at a third-grade level. I was addicted to cutting myself to relieve the pain and confusion that was in my body, and I was very sick from my eating disorder.

What I've Learned

It takes time to heal from years of secrets, trauma, and addiction. Starting the healing process requires a willingness to look at our past with an open heart, asking God what happened to us. Only then can we face our pain, fear, and abandonment issues and break free of the lies that our wounds tell us. This openness may mean admitting that our parents or caregivers were unable to provide for us emotionally, physically, financially, or spiritually.

Addiction is no respecter of person. It doesn't care what type of background you have, what degree you carry, or if you had praying parents. It affects so many people today in so many ways. Addiction comes to kill, steal, and destroy, and it will never make sense.

I had to admit what I went through as a child really *was* that bad. I had to let God in on the deepest secrets I never shared with anyone—all my struggles and pain. I had to talk to Him about my fear. I had to learn to be gentle with myself with all my ups and downs through the process. And while going through this, I had to learn to put up healthy boundaries

But at that moment in the closet, I felt a nudge telling me, *Don't give up.*

> **Starting the healing process requires a willingness to look at our past with an open heart, asking God what happened to us.**

by saying no to people so I could get the help I needed.

My faith played a huge role in my healing process and my recovery. Both my faith and my recovery program encouraged me to keep going and to never give up on myself. When I first heard the Scripture Jeremiah 29:11 (NLT), it prompted something in me to start asking questions and to start moving forward with action. The verse says, "For I know the plans I have for you,' says the Lord. 'They are plans for good and not for disaster, to give you a future and a hope.'"

The more help I got, the braver I became. And the stronger I got, the more changes I was able to make to better my life. The more I healed, the more determined I was to become the woman God created me to be. Over time I felt like my brain was starting to work again. I felt like I was coming out of a coma. I was becoming alive again and finding my true self. I no longer had to shut down all the time, because I was finding my voice and learning to discern what I needed in life.

 *Living Truth*

Guard your heart above all else, for it determines the course of your life. (Proverbs 4:23 NLT)

And everyone who has given up houses or brothers or sisters or father or mother or children or property, for my sake, will receive a hundred times as much in return and will have eternal life. (Matthew 19:29 NLT)

✑ Living Prayer

Imagine Jesus is sitting in the room with you. Even if you were like me in the beginning, and you are not sure if God exists, repeat this prayer by faith.

Dear God, I am tired of doing it my way. My way is no longer working, and it's not making my pain go away. I feel so tired and exhausted, and I am ready for peace and joy in my life. Please give me the willingness to do whatever it takes to heal and become a whole person. Right now, I am trusting You to heal all of me, my soul, and all my past wounds. I am asking You to forgive me for my sins. Please come live in my heart and take over my life. I am asking You by faith to bring the people, places, and resources I need to recover and become the person You created me to be.

The more I healed, the
more determined I was
to become the woman God
created me to be.

⤙ Living Action

- After reading parts of my story and my everyday struggles, can you relate to it in any way?
- Do you struggle with any secrets or some of the same beliefs that plagued me?
- Are there any areas of your life that you are trying to escape through some form of addiction or coping mechanism?
- Take some time right now to write out your answers. Be specific and honest with yourself.

_____

_____

_____

_____

_____

_____

_____

_____

_____

Paula Jauch is trauma survivor, motivational speaker, and author, who has a heart for the hurting. The words she shares are written from a place of brokenness and healing. She shares a message of hope and freedom all around the world. Her voice comes through loud and clear because she speaks bold truth. To learn more you can follow her on Instagram, Facebook, or Twitter (@paulajauch) and at paulajauch.com

Chapter Ten

Rolling Up My Sleeves

Sara Kennerley

I was stuck.

Because of the many scars littering my body, I was overwhelmed by shame associated with my appearance. Yes, I was a "new creation," redeemed from a ten-year battle with deep, despairing depression and extreme, excessive self-harm, but now I felt choked under a stranglehold of my new nemesis—shame.

The scars are gruesome and cover my hands and go upward along my arms on both sides, all the way up to my shoulders. Though now free from my battle with such dark depression, I felt like a walking caution sign on display to the world. My scars would always highlight my status as a walking disaster. Proceed carefully, folks! This girl is a mess!

How could I live victorious and free looking like this?

I longed to be normal and blend in with a world of seemingly confident, capable, and productive adults. I longed to know I had a place of value and meaning in their midst, and that I could accomplish something great still after years of emptiness and idleness when I was literally wasting away in my hopeless state of self-destruction.

I needed freedom from shame.

I felt choked under a stranglehold of my new nemesis—shame.

But for the time being, I hid. I accepted defeat at the hands of my nemesis, and I strove to press forward into my goals while wearing long sleeves at all times. My caution sign needed dimming, and this was the solution I could muster.

Even in the stifling heat of summer, I desperately clung to my mission to hide my scars. If ever there was a time to break free and renounce shame's hold on me, it was then. Yet I couldn't, not in my own strength. My closet may have been scattered with delightful little tank tops and tees from years past, but I wouldn't be enjoying them. I couldn't. I chose sweating and further suffering instead.

How odd a choice! I'd heard Jesus's voice speaking love and destiny over me in the middle of my brokenness. I'd witnessed God's redemption in my story and seen the miraculous work of restoration He'd begun. I was delivered from the death-grip of self-harm. I'd found a volunteer job I enjoyed, and it offered me hope and a potential career to pursue.

Yet here I was, stuck, overwhelmed by shame.

When at last I understood how profoundly sinister was my nemesis, and how profoundly more awesome was my God, I chose to pray. Sobbing at the feet of Jesus, I laid down my battle with shame. I hated that I'd come so far and yet was still so broken, so defined by my past brokenness.

Faithfully, Jesus met me there and offered me His hand up and out from my miry funk.

I was reminded of my friend Darren's coined phrase, "Sara, you've got to close that door if you want to see victory." As I pondered his words, I determined to indeed close the door of shame's chokehold over me.

In order to do that, I needed to release shame's controlling grip. I needed to roll up my sleeves—so that's what I did.

To say this step of faith was easy would be a lie. I was still terrified of feeling so exposed, so vulnerable. There were moments when I'd nearly vomit at the obvious wide-eyed stares and voiceless assumptions I believed would surely follow.

But as I continued to choose to stand strong, sleeves rolled up, the tormenting bile eventually subsided. Breathing deeply, the hard moments passed.

I'd closed the door. Another victory.

Now free of shame's grip, God can use me in and despite my visible brokenness.

I've been learning about the power of brokenness, and the power found in being okay with my weakness.

Paul's reminder in 2 Corinthians 12:9 (ESV) offers me hope when I feel insecure about my past and its evident physical display on my body: "But he said to me, 'My grace is sufficient for you, for my power is made perfect in weakness.' Therefore I will boast all the more gladly of my weaknesses, so that the power of Christ may rest upon me."

When I think about Christ's power, it makes me brave. It gets me excited. He healed the sick. He cast out demons. He defeated death entirely. Nothing is impossible for Him. That same power is at work within me as His daughter. Despite my brokenness. Despite my weakness. Even more so, in the midst of them!

The beauty of the gospel message is that I have never been deserving of God's love and mercy in my own strength, yet I am loved and offered mercy time and again. Scars and all.

As I continue to choose to roll up my sleeves, I get to witness Christ's power that rests on me and is at work in me and through me.

I've been able to share hope with others walking through their own brokenness by allowing these scars to point to Him. Our world is groaning, hungry for relief from the sorrow. People long to know there *is* hope beyond their current battles—whether internal or external.

Precious ones, our hope is found in Jesus.

It's humbling to think about my own ugly scars being a beacon of hope. In my years of despair, they were nothing more than grotesque wounds displaying my utter hopelessness. Now they are cracks in the clay jar of my being, used to shine the light of the glory of God into the world.

I'm reminded that God can't use me if I pretend to have it all together. To be a broken vessel on display, shining for Jesus and pointing others to Him, now *that* is the ultimate success. Anything I try and do in my own strength, while covering up my weakness and scars, will simply not be as beautiful or impactful.

Sobbing at the feet of Jesus, I laid down my battle with shame.

I'm blessed to have this opportunity, this life. I'm blessed to be free of shame's chokehold. I'm blessed when I roll up my sleeves. What was once a caution sign, God has turned into a beacon of light for His glory.

❧ Living Truth

For God, who said, "Let light shine out of darkness," has shone in our hearts to give the light of the knowledge of the glory of God in the face of Jesus Christ. But we have this treasure in jars of clay, to show that the surpassing power belongs to God and not to us. (2 Corinthians 4:6–7 ESV)

❧ Living Prayer

Lord Jesus, use me—this broken clay jar that I am—for Your glory. The scars life afford us pale in comparison to the beauty of who You are. Remind me that it's when I'm weak that You are strong. Give me strength to choose daily to roll up my sleeves and allow the world to see my brokenness. Only then will they see You—the One who heals and redeems what's lost and broken. Oh, that the world would know You and the hope found in You. Thank You for delighting in me just as I am, and giving me beauty in place of my ashes.

It's humbling to think
about my own ugly scars
being a beacon of hope.

～ *Living Action*

- Where have you seen evidence of God's redemption of the brokenness and scars in your life?
- Are there parts of your story that still stir up shame and fear within you?
- How might you *roll up your sleeves* and choose to stand on the truth of God's Word instead?

_____

_____

_____

_____

_____

_____

_____

_____

_____

_____

Sara Kennerley has two little angels who call her "Mama" and her first boyfriend, turned husband, by her side. She is passionate about encouraging others and pointing them to the hope found in Jesus after being set free from a ten-year mental health crisis. Visit Sara's blog at withinthis jarofclay.com, and find her at Facebook.com/sarakennerleywriter and sara kennerley.com.

Chapter Eleven

Finding Freedom from Formidable Food
Christine Trimpe

Church, I have a confession. Please forgive my cracking voice. Speaking the truth out loud for the first time stirs up decades of buried emotion. Might as well hand me a tissue too. Here goes.

I am a food addict.

There, I said it.

I'm opening up these wounds to share the hope found in Jesus in overcoming our addictions: whether it be salty and sugary snacks, shoes, shopping, sex, or success. This is my story about the freedom I found in beating my decades-long addiction.

Because, church, I love you. And we need to talk about this hard stuff—these sins we often overlook.

I see the struggle and the heartbreak, and I know you wish you could break down the walls of addiction to break free from those chains once and for all. I hope my God story will inspire and encourage your heart.

I mourned for decades in despair as a result of my choices. As a food addict for almost fifty years, I found myself trapped in a vicious cycle. I craved carbohydrates and sugar, ate more than I intended, and stuffed myself until I felt miserably

Food literally separated me from the only One capable to rescue me from this addiction.

sick. Recently, I discovered that my high carbohydrate diet created this cycle of sugar cravings and sugar crashing. All day, every day. Stuffing myself with carbs satisfied my body physiologically and psychologically.

In addition to the physical damage, emotionally I carried guilt and shame. I easily made excuses for my poor health and dieting failures. Most of the time I hid my excessive eating from my family. I hit up fast food drive-through windows alone and ate when everyone left the room, keeping my problem under wraps, or so I thought.

The painful truth? I checked off all the classic signs of food addiction.

Here's another hard truth, church. I *idolized* food.

I controlled my emotions and soothed my soul with food. Food filled the holes in my heart and soul while leaving them, plus my body and mind, severely damaged. I prioritized food over everything—especially the scant time spent in relationship with the very One who designed our physical need for food. Until recently, I have spent my entire adult life completely missing the mark on a deep and abiding relationship with Jesus because of my soul-sucking relationship with food. Food literally separated me from the only One capable to rescue me from this addiction.

I believe Paul understood my struggles when he wrote about the cravings of the flesh in his letter to the Ephesians regarding their former ways: "All of us also lived among them at one time, gratifying the cravings of our flesh and following its desires and thoughts" (Ephesians 2:3 NIV).

For decades the truth of my addiction weighed heavily on my body; my body that was a hundred pounds overweight revealed this truth. But harder to detect, the heavy weight also crushed my spirit. I wore masks to fiercely protect my heart, mind, and soul. In addition to shame and guilt, I struggled with insecurity, isolation, worthlessness, fear, and depression. My whole self languished in misery.

There were deeply painful times in my years of food addiction when I longed to check out of this life. I had no hope, no energy, no joy; surely my family would function without me. Eternal sleep sounded like the perfect escape from my chronic exhaustion. Praise God, He had other plans and never allowed me to see these plans from the Enemy through to an end.

In the late fall of 2015, I received three diagnoses that were concerning: I was morbidly obese and had obstructive sleep apnea, painful ovarian cysts, and non-alcoholic fatty liver disease (which may progress to cirrhosis of the liver).

The idea of an early death scared me to death. I guess I didn't really want to die an early death. In my despair, I cried out to Jesus for healing. He answered, just like He promised, and lifted me up from my miry pit and placed my feet on a firm foundation (Psalm 40).

Heavy chains of food addiction had ruled my life for decades. "Jesus, are You ready, willing, and able to do some heavy lifting? I lack strength. I need You!" I cried in my desperate prayers for healing.

He graciously reminded me time and time again to lay down my heavy burden, and He would give me one thing I craved in my chronic exhaustion—rest. Ah, rest! His yoke is easy, and His burden is light (Matthew 11:30). I took a bold step in trusting Him for a miracle and marveled as He did the heavy lifting without missing a step.

Why did I neglect His promise for decades? Food addiction is a formidable enemy. Let's face it—we have to eat, right? And comfort food is—you guessed it!—comforting. But here's the uncomfortable reality. My food addiction fast-tracked me to an early death and an empty life.

I needed a battle plan, and He delivered the perfect strategy. I found my hope by seeking answers in His Word. Every morning, without fail, I equip my battle with His promises and truth.

In his letter to the Ephesians, Paul went on to encourage the believers that we find living hope when we turn fleshly cravings over to a gracious God. He writes, "But because of his great love for us, God, who is rich in mercy, made us alive with Christ even when we were dead in transgressions—it is by grace you have been saved" (Ephesians 2:4–5 NIV).

As my spiritual journey with Jesus matured, I identified the true source of

> I took a bold step in trusting Him for a miracle and marveled as He did the heavy lifting without missing a step.

> Leaning into Jesus every day through His Word strengthened my resolve to cling to His Spirit of power and self-control.

hope for healing. Leaning into Jesus every day through His Word strengthened my resolve to cling to His Spirit of power and self-control. I waged war on the overwhelming cravings. I ditched the fear of failure and exposure and began the hard work of trusting His promises, covered in His love. Another verse penned by Paul equipped me in this battle: "For God gave us a spirit not of fear but of power and love and self-control" (2 Timothy 1:7 ESV).

Paul's wisdom encouraged me in weakness. Bone weary and weak for almost thirty years, I grasped Jesus's power to battle my weakness. I know in my weakness, His power is made strong (2 Corinthians 12:9). Jesus instilled in me the power to quit sugar. Within a few short weeks of my decision to quit sugar, the cravings were gone—a complete removal of my physical cravings for the substance that was destroying my health. Those powerful cravings for sugar and carbohydrates subsided and were overpowered by His Spirit of self-control.

After thirty years of failure, Jesus gifted me with a successful weight-loss journey and healed my obesity, chronic exhaustion, obstructive sleep apnea, ovarian cysts, fatty liver disease, prediabetes, mood disorders, and much more.

But I like to call these physical results just the side benefits on this joyful journey of healing. The true victory is found in my emotional and spiritual healing with Jesus. My chains of food addiction are gone—freeing my whole self to serve Him with a revived zeal for life.

I gained this freedom by wholly committing to my walk with Him, abiding with Him in His Word, allowing His sanctifying process to create me in His image.

I have been freed from my sinful cravings.

Freed from idolatry of food.

All by His power—and His beautiful gift of self-control.

Church, Jesus is waiting to break your chains of addiction and idolatry. There is hope here: "And call upon me in the day of trouble; I will deliver you, and you shall glorify me" (Psalm 50:15 ESV).

I give Him all the glory for my rescue. *One thing* wholly fills the holes in my soul. One thing I now crave—the Bread of Life, Jesus.

I am free.

⤳ *Living Truth*

So if the Son sets you free, you will be free indeed. (John 8:36 ESV)

⤳ *Living Prayer*

Powerful and mighty Lord, thank You for loving and creating me in Your image for a purpose. Walk with me daily while I make moment-by-moment decisions about feeding my body, mind, heart, and soul. Thank You for the gift of the spirit of self-control and the promise of Your power and strength to cover me in my weakness. Help me break the strongholds in my life for Your glory. I surrender to Your will and Your perfect plan for my physical, emotional, and spiritual health and wellness. You promise that nothing is impossible and every chain is breakable. In You I will celebrate my victory over earthly addictions. You and only You are my living hope.

～ *Living Action*

- Inspect your heart and soul for holes.
- How are you filling these holes? Food, shopping, gossip, schedules, materialism, work, internet, gambling, sex, drugs, alcohol?
- Are you ready to confess and trust Jesus to break the chains of your addictive behaviors separating you from the power, love, and self-control He freely offers you?

_____

_____

_____

_____

_____

_____

_____

_____

_____

_____

_____

_____

Christine Trimpe is a worship leader, writer, speaker, and joy seeker. Recently, God flipped the cravings of her soul and called her to inspire, motivate, and encourage others to pursue their best health: physically, emotionally, and spiritually. Her transformation story and social media links can be found at ChristineTrimpe.com.

Chapter Twelve

The Long Reach of Addiction
Rev. Jennifer Sakata

A raucous housewarming lit up the dark two nights earlier. No kids allowed. I stayed at a friend's house and came back "home" in the early morning to find cigarette butts, stogies, bottles, and the remnants of uneaten food littered all over our newly mortgaged, tiny shack of a house. I remember looking down at the dew on the grains of wood on the picnic table. Crying on the inside, but attempting boldness on the outside, I drew out a letter. I had written a few simple words with a shaky heart, instructing my mother, who should have been instructing me, on the dangers of alcohol and addiction.

Growing up in a troubled home resulted in some troubled thinking along the way to life with Jesus. It is a well-known adage that children of alcoholics typically grow either into perfectionists or rebels. I was a straight-A student, a talented flute player, a decent athlete, and liked by all my teachers, so you know which road I traveled.

Jesus became my Savior at an early age, but working hard, being the "best" Christian, and showing the world everything was fine, were the true sources of my hope. Sunday school teachers taught me Jesus is the way, the truth, and the life, but survival in my house taught me something different.

When the mind's secret hope is self, the spirit trips over insecurity, insignificance, and a paralyzing lack of self-worth. I just worked harder, determined to make things better and shine more brightly, even as I crumbled on the inside under the weight. Surrounded by the sin of another's addiction, and not yet surrendered to Christ's lordship in my life, I simply set myself up for my *own* addiction—to perfectionism, control, and hyperproductivity. I'm not sure there is a DSM-5 diagnostic code for mental disorders for that, but my addiction, and maybe yours, was no less real.

I was sixteen and attending a winter camp with my youth group when a teenage girl with an incredible voice sang "The Via Dolorosa" (which means "the way of suffering") by Sandi Patty. I heard in the haunting melody how for so many years, I had depended only on myself. As the words told of Christ's love that caused Him to walk the way of suffering for me, they landed like heavy drops of rain, with power to loosen the grasp of my own hard-packed addiction to self. I clung to my accomplishments like a child whose grip to her blankie is unyielding when her mama wants to wash it. I saw clearly how I proclaimed Jesus as Savior with my mouth, but kept Him far from lordship in my life.

That's what addiction does. It creates a false reality, just close enough to the truth that you don't see it for the lie it is. Without being Lord in my life, Jesus couldn't really be my Savior.

I made a commitment to follow Jesus that weekend, as Lord and leader of my life. Christ suffered once for all on the cross, and He just wants me to be found and free and whole, living daily marinated in hope in Him—not hope in me.

The apostle Paul wrote Romans as an articulation of his faith in Christ. He doesn't mince words about our egregious offense to God because of the filth of our sin. "For everyone has sinned; we all fall short of God's glorious standard" (Romans 3:23 NLT). We may clothe ourselves with the appearance of strength and significance, but God is not deceived by appearances. Nor is God confused about our need for His Son's

Sunday school teachers taught me Jesus is the way, the truth, and the life, but survival in my house taught me something different.

forgiveness. "The wages of sin is death" (Romans 6:23 NLT). We cannot save ourselves. There is no hope living in us when addiction to anything is working throughout us.

So God, in His mercy and kindness, invites us to living hope in life with

> I saw clearly how I proclaimed Jesus as Savior with my mouth, but kept Him far from lordship in my life.

Jesus. God invites us to be forgiven, freed, and released to follow a new voice over the old voices, capable only of bondage and unrelenting disappointments. Living hope begins to unravel the lies, loosen the compulsions, and undo the patterns of production that leave us empty, never satisfied, and always demanding more. Paul said, "Yet God in His grace, freely makes us right in his sight. He did this through Christ Jesus when he freed us from the penalty for our sins" (Romans 3:24 NLT). With no help from us, the grasp of addiction is thrown as far as the east is from the west.

Our salvation comes as source and substance of living hope in our here and now. When the grab of addictive tendencies reaches to pull us back, the work of living hope lifts the head, puts a sparkle in the eyes, and takes the heaviness of this life and rests it in the big enough hands of the God of all hope. Where addiction strangles and poisons everyone and everything it touches, living hope infuses joy, strengthens the weary, encourages the tired and gives rightly placed confidence to those who would risk trusting God with the expectation of fulfillment.

This living hope isn't wishful thinking or life made easy in an instant. Living hope requires a steadfastness of spirit that trusts in what cannot be seen right away. It summons the endurance of a marathon runner, who envisions the finish line far down the road but puts in the discipline and the sweat to run one mile at a time. Living hope demands we put aside our ingrained perceptions of our "best life now, as I've earned it" in exchange for what will be, because God has designed it and freed us to live it. Living hope doesn't make all struggles or difficulties disappear. But it is the resounding voice of God who tells us He has made us and called us by name. He has prepared us for a plan and a purpose, not of our choosing, but of His working, for our good and His glory.

> Living hope begins to unravel the lies, loosen the compulsions, and undo the patterns of production that leave us empty, never satisfied, and always demanding more.

It's been a lifetime since I stood trembling by that dewy picnic table with its distinctive grains of wood. I didn't know then what I know now: addiction has a long reach. My addiction didn't come sealed in a bottle or rolled in a joint. Addiction seeped in through the guise of self-propelled perfection, control, and hyperproductivity. While addiction does have a long reach, God's arms stretch further.

Mercifully, God had other plans for me, as I know He has for You. He gave me living hope in place of dead-end production, living hope in exchange for controlling compulsions and the pursuit of perfect. His living hope is rooted in Jesus and lived out in real life, one moment at a time.

Living Truth

Therefore, since we have been made right in God's sight by faith, we have peace with God because of what Jesus Christ our Lord has done for us. Because of our faith, Christ has brought us into this place of undeserved privilege, where we now stand, and we confidently and joyfully look forward to sharing God's glory. We can rejoice too, when we run into problems and trials, for we know that they help us develop endurance. And endurance develops strength of character, and character strengthens our confident hope of salvation. And this hope will not lead to disappointment. For we know how dearly God loves us, because He has given us the Holy Spirit to fill our hearts with His love. (Romans 5:3–5 NLT)

Living Prayer

Long-reaching God, You see clearly the things that reach out to capture me and hold me locked up. You know the size and shape of my captors—the ones in my mind, the ones that seep into my heart, and the ones that threaten to undo all You've given for my good and Your glory. To You, Lord, I return myself. Give me only Your love and Your grace. Living in hope, that is enough for me.

Living Action

- Identify two or three areas in which you are secretly pinning your hopes on yourself.
- In what ways are you discreetly addicted or quietly captive to what you may accomplish for yourself? Bring those areas to Jesus in prayer. Confess specifically and reread prayerfully Romans 5:3–5.

While addiction does have a long reach, God's arms stretch further.

- Identify two or three local women whose lives model living hope to you. Where do you see Jesus at work in them? How do they live? What words do they use? What words do others use about them? After you reflect, pray for them. Invite them to coffee or lunch.

_____

_____

_____

_____

_____

_____

_____

_____

_____

_____

Rev. Jennifer Sakata is a storyteller, observer of life, and redeemed daughter of the King. She lives in Central Illinois with her husband Craig and their two comical sons. She is active in their community, and you might even catch her cycling on her pink-tired road bike. Connect with Jennifer on Facebook and through her blog, Grace Through a Not so Perfect Pot, at jennifersakata.com.

Part 3

Abuse

Chapter Thirteen

3 Things I Learned from 12 Years of Spiritual Abuse and Manipulation

Athena Dean Holtz

Convinced we were on the eve of destruction called Y2K, my husband and I wanted to prepare for the worst. So we moved in July of 1999 from one end of Western Washington to the other, to Enumclaw, a small self-contained town. Not long after that, one of our publishing company's newer authors, whose wife I met at a Christian writers' conference, sent us an audio tape of his sermon entitled "Praise God for Y2K." His hard-hitting and persuasive message was a completely different perspective, and we were both intrigued. That began a journey into deception that lasted nearly thirteen years.

It started with a claim that he'd found a truth we wouldn't hear anywhere else. Anyone in agreement with his "truth" showed they truly loved God and were on the "narrow road." All other churches were on the "wide road that led to destruction" (Matthew 7:13).

It wasn't long before we were convinced to cut off any friends or family who did not go along with this "truth," or were divisive. Of course, anyone who questioned his doctrine was divisive and had to be cut off.

Thus began the systematic disowning of my children and then divorcing my husband (all in the name of Jesus, mind you) as they all "turned against" God by

I'd spent almost thirteen years following a lie that I believed to be the truth.

criticizing and attacking this wonderful ministry. (Can you hear the sarcasm in my voice?)

I was all in, absolutely sure *they* were in sin, and *I* was seeing clearly God's work that needed to be done. We were opening the eyes of those deceived by a worldly Christianity. I now had the truth, and it was worth giving up everything dear to me to see this "truth" proclaimed. A worthy cause, I thought. So worthy, I was eventually willing to turn over my twenty-year-old publishing company to help in that effort. Oh, how wrong I was!

On November 10, 2011, something finally clicked in my heart. The realization that I'd been duped by a con man washed over me like molten lava. I'd spent almost thirteen years following a lie that I believed to be the truth. I'd lost everything that mattered to me, and I'd lost it all through major deception and spiritual abuse. I was a victim, but I soon learned I was not innocent.

As I began to unpack the poor choices I'd made in my incredibly misguided zeal, I asked a question that created a defining moment in my life.

"Lord, what was wrong with me? What door did I open to the Evil One to get to a place where I believed a lie was the truth and gave up everything for it?"

What He showed me next rocked my world and set my healing path on an expedited timetable.

No Foundation

He took me back to my salvation experience, and how quickly I ended up in full-time ministry, never taking the time to learn to be a Berean—those who receive the Word with eagerness but also examine it daily to see if what they are being taught is true. I hadn't learned the difference between Scripture in context and out of context. That one thing right there cost me dearly.

Those who abuse others in the name of Jesus use Scripture out of context to push their agendas—divide marriages, families, and friends—in order to isolate victims and keep them buying into the leaders' doctrine. A high level of intimidation is present to keep followers from asking questions, challenging the use of Scripture, or pointing out error.

As one who dreads conflict and avoids it regularly, allowing myself to be manipulated with Scripture out of context was a natural result of my weakness. It didn't help that I was also very weak in my knowledge of Scripture.

Vulnerable from Wounding

I spent many years teaching women the importance of self-care. As I ministered to wives of Vietnam veterans in the late 80s and early 90s, I discovered many women married to a vet had PTSD of their own from childhood trauma. The veterans didn't have a corner on the market.

As much as I taught others that we needed to allow God into those broken areas of our lives, I avoided ever letting Him into those walled-off parts of my heart. That left me vulnerable. I used work as my medication of choice to dull the pain from childhood sexual abuse, an abortion at age nineteen, domestic violence, divorce, and more. Because I self-medicated, I was not emotionally healthy, did not have good boundaries, and was easily deceived. I am convinced con men have a built-in radar enabling them to pick out people who are broken and in denial and then reel them into their webs.

Lack of Trust = Compromise

When I decided to publish this false teacher's manuscript, my editor begged me, "Please, Athena, don't publish this! It will cause division." I did not want to hear that. This author was going to publish five thousand copies of his book, and that was a sizeable order. I'd already made my list of all the bills I was going to pay with that income. I didn't trust

> As one who dreads conflict and avoids it regularly, allowing myself to be manipulated with Scripture out of context was a natural result of my weakness.

God to provide another source of income to pay those bills, so I hardened my heart. Greed led to lack of trust. Lack of trust led to compromise. I made the decision to publish something that was doctrinally suspect in order to pay my business bills instead of trusting God to provide a way of escape.

Realizing that while I was a victim, I had also contributed to the deception helped me gain valuable perspective. I couldn't just point the finger at the "pastor" and his wife for the years of spiritual abuse, I had to point the finger at myself for my ignorance, my unhealed trauma, and my greed and lack of trust. That changed the trajectory of my healing and brought God's redemption into my life in breath-taking ways.

One thing you can be sure of, God never squanders our troubles. As we begin to connect the dots to see where we've ignored the caution signs He's sent our way, He is always faithful to forgive us, correct, admonish, and instruct us so we learn from our pain and grow. Then He will bring others into our lives who've experienced something similar, so we can help them on their healing journeys. What a gift it is to be Jesus "with skin on" and offer the same comfort He's sent our way.

```
As much as I taught
others that we needed
to allow God into those
broken areas of our
lives, I avoided ever
letting Him into those
walled-off parts of my
heart.
```

∼ *Living Truth*

He comforts us every time we have trouble, so when others have trouble, we can comfort them with the same comfort God gives us. (2 Corinthians 1:4 NCV)

Realizing that while I was a victim, I had also contributed to the deception helped me gain valuable perspective.

∼ *Living Prayer*

Oh Lord, please help me see where I am in spiritual deception and guide me on my way back to You. I choose to allow You into my areas of wounding so You can heal my heart. Help me take responsibility for the part I played in my detour into deception. Allow me to extend the same comfort to others You have given to me.

❧ Living Action

- Have you ever found yourself facing the consequences of your own bad choices and wondered, *How did I get here?*
- Or have you struggled with coming to the place of ownership over your choices, preferring to blame others for the fallout you face?
- What is God saying to you about your part in the spiritual abuse you endured?

_____

_____

_____

_____

_____

_____

_____

_____

_____

_____

Athena Dean Holtz serves as the publisher of Redemption Press and founder of the She Writes for Him movement. Her memoir, *Full Circle: Coming Home to the Faithfulness of God* tells her story of overcoming severe spiritual abuse. Past president of the Northwest Christian Writers Association, former radio host of Always Faithful, and host of the Redeemed & Restored Podcast, she is married to Dr. Ross Holtz, founding pastor of The Summit EFC in Enumclaw, Washington.

Chapter Fourteen

Behind the Mask
Cherie Denna

The reflection of sound from the news reporter's announcement to "shelter in place" due to COVID-19, bounced from our farmhouse walls. Shock drew me to attention in the center of our living room.

"Something is wrong," I said to my husband, looking him in the eye. "This isn't right."

My response did not come from a place of rational thinking and logic; it came from a completely different place. My mind raced as trembling and nausea accompanied my increased heart rate. *Nobody is going to tell me I cannot leave my home. They are trying to control us. Over my dead body!* Tense with fear, my fight-or-flight response kicked in. There was something evil behind the announcement, I just knew it.

I have suffered with symptoms of complex post-traumatic stress disorder (C-PTSD) for as far back as I can remember. My parents and family of outlaws conditioned me to never trust anyone outside the family, especially the government or law enforcement. I *was* to trust my pedophile stepfather.

When Jesus rescued me from that life, He set me on a course of emotional healing and spiritual deliverance. Counseling for survivors of childhood trauma, prayer

My parents and family of outlaws conditioned me to never trust anyone outside the family, especially the government or law enforcement.

counseling, and faith-based recovery programs all contributed to the present state of my mental health. But the ebbs and flows of C-PTSD symptoms have no regard for our spiritual rebirth. It was a reality while writing about past trauma, and it was proven again when our world was jerked from beneath our feet with the COVID-19 pandemic.

We never saw it coming. In our effort to make sense of conflicting reports, we searched the internet for truth. Isolation took its toll on our souls. We soon found ourselves in a surge of a mental health storm some believe to be more catastrophic than COVID-19 itself.

The war over face masks became a marker for some in determining good from evil. Accusations flew between friends. We were given the evil eye if our choices differed. We pointed fingers at an invisible enemy, which for many was like something from a movie. We wrestled not against flesh and blood. We bit our tongue to avoid conflict. Some of us screamed from the top of our lungs, "I won't be silenced!" or "I will continue to sing from behind my mask!"

What does God see behind your mask? When He looks at me, He sees a fragile soul standing strong in His truth. He sees through my mask, directly into my heart.

Maybe when He sees my friend, He sees someone who is overcome with disappointment. Her hope in her fellow brothers and sisters in Christ is shattered. She is appalled they do not speak with a calming balm of encouragement in the Lord. Our humanness is too much for her.

But the compassion of the Lord intervenes. He says, "Above all else, guard your heart, for everything you do flows from it" (Proverbs 4:23 NIV).

I think God sees heart-wrenching brokenness behind the masks and whispers,

> Trust in the Lord and do good. Then you will live safely in the land and prosper. Take delight in the Lord, and He will give you your heart's desires. Commit everything you do to the Lord. Trust him,

and He will help you. He will make your innocence radiate like the dawn, and the justice of your cause will shine like the noonday sun. Be still in the presence of the Lord and wait patiently for Him to act. Don't worry about evil people who prosper or fret about their wicked schemes. (Psalm 37:3–7 NLT)

Tending to my soul includes frequent intimate time with the Lord at the seashore. It is what I call my "seahabilitation," and it is a requirement for managing my mental health. I also must remain attentive to the amount of data I absorb each day, remaining informed yet not consumed by the world. Understanding the boundaries of my mental health helps me manage it.

How do you guard your thoughts and tend to your soul wounds?

God has determined that His people will not be spared the tragedies of the world. Scripture describes many threatening and overwhelming life events. Though C-PTSD is not given a name in the Scriptures, we read of women like Mary Magdalene, who Jesus delivered from seven demons (Luke 8:1–2). Do you ever wonder what her life must have been like before that day? I imagine she endured much trauma. We do not know exactly how the demons tormented her, but the Bible describes persons afflicted with demons as characterized by being tormented. That is quite different from living in willful rebellion to God. They were often outcasts of society and were miserable, sorrowful, lonely people.

Experiencing undeniable hope, abundant joy, and true belonging was most likely unheard of for Mary Magdalene. Imagine the transformation in her countenance! It is no wonder no woman in the Bible superseded Mary Magdalene in her utter devotion to Jesus. He saw behind her spiritual mask of affliction. She never shifted her focus away from her Lord and Savior.

What about the woman with the issue of blood for over twelve years (Leviticus 15:19–28) who, in her despair, reached out to get just one touch of the hem of Jesus's garment? Isolated due to her impurity, she was not meant to touch *anyone*, not even her husband. It was being almost as good as dead. She looked upon Jesus and

He sees through my mask, directly into my heart.

believed that He was who He claimed to be, the Messiah. She believed if she could only touch Him, she would be healed.

Jesus saw behind her mask of physical affliction. "Jesus turned around and spoke to her. 'Daughter,' he said, 'all is well! Your faith has healed you.' And the woman was well from that moment" (Matthew 9:22 TLB).

I am in the process of writing my memoir, *Biker Blood: An Outcast's Quest for Justice and Belonging*, my hard Romans 8:28 story. Delving into those dark times in order to show the glory that came from them takes a toll on me, emotionally and spiritually.

God met me on one of my coastal writing getaways. That weekend I would write the most difficult chapter of the book. I would revisit scenes of sexual abuse that my sister and I experienced at the hands of our stepfather. Feelings of guilt returned as I thought about my sister.

Before setting out to write, I prayed, "God, I'm not sure how I found the strength at times. It had to be You. There is no other explanation."

On the second day, I realized it was August 28—my stepfather's birthday. It was also Romans 8:28 Day. I shook my head in wonder. *Oh Lord, Your timing is so perfect. You ordain my steps. You are writing this story.*

When a friend posted on social media that it was *her* birthday, she referred to her 8:28 birth Scripture, "And we know that in all things God works for the good of those who love him, who have been called according to his purpose" (Romans 8:28 NIV). I loved the idea of a birth Scripture. I opened my Bible app. Hmm, I wonder what my birth Scripture is for 4/17?

I researched 4:17 passages from each book of the Bible. When I came to 2 Timothy 4:17 (NIV), there it was: "But the Lord stood at my side and gave me strength, so that through me the message might be fully proclaimed and all the Gentiles might hear it. And I was delivered from the lion's mouth."

> God has determined that His people will not be spared the tragedies of the world.

Sensing the Father's presence, I closed my eyes and prayed. "Thank You for meeting me here and giving me the strength. Thank You for hearing my prayer and for Your blessed assurance.

Thank You for a clear mind and for Your protection as I write."

Oh Lord, Your timing is so perfect. You ordain my steps. You are writing this story.

I knew God must have been watching over me before I knew Him. I believe with all my heart that only by His power could I be delivered from the grip of evil. But this sealed it.

The Enemy loves to influence our emotions with spiritual battles raging around us every single day. We know he *is* a roaring lion, prowling around looking for someone to devour (1 Peter 5:8). When Satan's demons attempt to influence our emotions, we have a choice to either fall prey to their tactics or be filled with encouragement through the Word of God. Peter tells us the Enemy tries to take out as many Christians as possible, and even cause us to walk away from Christ. "Resist him, standing firm in the faith, because you know that the family of believers throughout the world is undergoing the same kind of sufferings" (1 Peter 5:9 NIV).

Those words help me see my loved ones through God's lens behind their masks and to pray for them accordingly.

⤳ *Living Truth*

But the Lord stood by me and strengthened and empowered me, so that through me the [gospel] message might be fully proclaimed, and that all the Gentiles might hear it; and I was rescued from the mouth of the lion. The Lord will rescue me from every evil assault, and He will bring me safely into His heavenly kingdom; to Him be the glory forever and ever. Amen. (2 Timothy 4:17–18 AMP)

Living Prayer

God of Abraham, Isaac, and Jacob, I praise You for who You are. You know every thought and every word even before it is spoken. Your thoughts of me outnumber the grains of sand on the seashore. Thank You, Lord, for keeping Your hand upon me through the darkest moments of my life. Draw me to Your truth so I may renounce the lies of the Enemy when they attack my mind. Renew my mind each day with Your Word and the power of Your Spirit. Lord, sing over me as I sleep, so I may wake with a song on my heart.

Show me how to look behind the masks of those You place in my path. Give me a compassionate and discerning heart toward all. I break the power of the Enemy over my life, in Jesus's name. I declare and decree that every curse that the Enemy and his agents are trying to reinforce in my life are null and void. I paralyze all the works of the Enemy over my life. Help me live devoted to only Your truth, God. May my allegiance never waver. Guard my heart and mind and keep me in perfect peace as my mind remains focused on You. My trust is only in You. I praise You and surrender all these things to You.

When Satan's demons attempt to influence our emotions, we have a choice to either fall prey to their tactics or be filled with encouragement through the Word of God.

~ Living Action

- How has the COVID-19 pandemic impacted your mental and/or spiritual health? List three ways.
- Commit to adopting ways to improve your mental health and tending to your soul. What three ideas come to mind?

_____

_____

_____

_____

_____

_____

_____

_____

_____

_____

_____

_____

Cherie Denna is an author, blogger, and writer of devotionals. Her published works include contributions to Janet Thompson's *Everyday Brave: Living Courageously as a Woman of Faith* and the *Inspire Grace* anthology. Her upcoming memoir is *Biker Blood: An Outcast's Quest for Justice and Belonging*. Cherie enjoys life with her husband in northern California. Connect with her at cheriedenna.com and on Facebook and Instagram.

Chapter Fifteen

What Did I Get Myself Into?
Maureen Hager

I fixed my gaze on the poster near the door. It read "Thou Shall Not Hassle." Viggo, high on methamphetamines, pinned me against the wall and shoved a loaded pistol between my legs. I had no idea why he was so angry, but I knew better than to provoke him. I was his wife, his old lady, and his property. He gave the orders, and I obeyed.

Thankfully, something distracted him, and he stumbled away. As soon as he loosened his grip, I grabbed my keys and ran to my car. My body was shaking; my mind flashed images of what could have happened. The truth is, I had nowhere to go.

Growing up, a lack of emotional security at home caused me to search for love and acceptance outside my family. This misguided search lured me into a world of drugs and life in a motorcycle gang. I envisioned myself as part of this outlaw family, pledging my loyalty to them.

I quickly learned that gang life is not a lifestyle but a way of life. Any ties with family or friends outside the club must be severed. It was an illusion of freedom that required adopting a lifestyle of rebellion against the mainstream culture.

I quickly learned that gang life is not a lifestyle but a way of life.

Women take up with bikers for different reasons. They come from all walks of life. Some women are abducted, but most attach themselves voluntarily to the club and everything it stands for—drugs, parties, excitement, fast bikes, and a sense of belonging. Women must be outwardly submissive and never negotiate or question their old man's demands. They are expected to work and bring all their income to their old man. Outlaw biker gangs consider women second-class citizens.

Viggo's unpredictable acts of violence invited retaliation from a rival gang. My house was ransacked, and many of my possessions were stolen. The next night as Viggo walked toward our van, he was attacked from behind, knocked unconscious, and kidnapped to New York City. Angels must have guarded my doorway because the gang members never came to the house. I could have been violently raped and beaten.

I soon developed a false sense of security. It wasn't until I witnessed many injustices against others that I realized I was slipping into a dark world without hope. An old lady could be beaten by her old man for any reason, and others were forbidden to intercede. Viggo's destructive forces of control and dominance left me powerless to live in any kind of freedom. I had no idea how I would escape from the power the gang imposed on my life.

My answer came most unexpectedly. In the early morning hours, a rival gang armed with M16 rifles stood outside the clubhouse where we lived. I was standing in the doorway facing the front windows and silhouetted by light when the shooting started.

As I reached for the light switch, I felt a fiery sensation in my left forearm that covered my heart. I have no explanation as to why I used my left arm to turn on the light since the switch was to my right. The Lord was my shield that night; He protected me from the gang that came to kill and destroy.

The impact of the bullets threw me face down. Before I hit the floor, another bullet lodged in my right thigh. My left arm had been blown apart, and the bone in my leg was shattered. The bedroom blinds lay ripped open; glass fragments covered the floor. The shooting continued; I could not move.

Hours later, I awoke in the intensive care unit to the sounds of beeping machines surrounding me. My right knee had pins surgically inserted into the bone; my leg hung suspended in traction. My left arm was covered in a plaster cast. Viggo was nowhere to be found.

For six months, my hospital bed was my home. Intense pain became a constant companion. When the bones in my leg did not fuse, the next attempt at repair was to put me in a body cast. I lay in a cocoon of plaster for the next two months.

The results of additional tests confirmed the bones in my leg and arm were too shattered to be reconnected. Surgery was scheduled for the next day to fuse the bones in my leg together using a bone fragment from my right hip.

That night Viggo came to visit me. He told me he was leaving town in the morning to take care of club business. I begged him to stay, but he refused. I never saw him again.

The surgery left my leg two inches shorter. I was transported back home and started a year of intense therapy. Viggo never contacted me, although I had numerous brothers call to ask me to be their old lady. I knew if I was to change, I needed to sever all ties with the gang. None of them could ever be the family I longed to have.

Recovering from the trauma of physical, emotional, and spiritual brokenness became a long and arduous journey. At times, I questioned whether I could ever be whole again. Today I have a limited range of motion in my arm and leg. Gradually, I learned to live with my disabilities.

When a former biker friend invited me to attend a baptismal service at her church, I agreed to go because of the transformation I saw in her. Listening to the testimonies of others, the good news of the gospel filled my heart with hope. That night I asked Jesus to be my Lord and Savior. I learned deliverance and restoration come to those who open their heart to the Redeemer and Savior, Jesus Christ. He longs for each of us to have a personal encounter with Him.

The truth is, brokenness is a reality for all of us. We will all experience the pain and suffering of a broken heart. The

I had no idea how I would escape from the power the gang imposed on my life.

degrees of heartache will vary, but we have a choice to stay in our brokenness or to receive the Lord's restoration.

I've discovered the best way to heal a broken heart is to give God all the pieces. Despite the circumstances and trials in our lives, God wants to provide us with the freedom of wholeness. One of the ways we find His freedom is through forgiveness. Forgiving someone does not mean what they did was okay. Forgiveness does require a willingness to open old wounds and let God show you the offending person as He sees them.

Forgiving Viggo seemed impossible. He didn't deserve my forgiveness. He put my life in danger, he neglected me, he dishonored me, and he abandoned me in the hospital. The crippling bullets forever changed my life. It turns out Viggo knew the rival gang that shot me. It was a payback hit of retaliation to protect their territory. Viggo didn't physically pull the trigger, but he was the catalyst behind the bullets. Many times, I asked the Lord to help me forgive him. I wanted the Lord's restoration in my life. With each conscious act of forgiveness, I loosened the destructive grip Viggo held over my life.

Jesus is called a Man of Sorrows. He knows your pain and can empathize with you. Jesus was broken for you. His finished work on the cross secured your hope. There is hope in the valley. There is deliverance at the end of each trial. There is joy in the journey.

Our past does not define us. Instead, Jesus offers us a new life in Him. "Therefore, if anyone is in Christ, he is a new creation; old things have passed away; behold, all things have become new" (2 Corinthians 5:17 NKJV).

Give the Lord the key to your heart. Allow God to carry your burdens, your pain, your loneliness, and your regrets. The brokenness in my life became the key that unlocked the treasures of the love I sought—the love of the Father. His love gave me the courage to hope, to live, and to love again.

For six months, my hospital bed was my home. Intense pain became a constant companion.

Healing is possible. By surrendering your will and trusting Him with your future, you will find true freedom in His plan for your life. "For I know the thoughts that I think toward you, says the LORD, thoughts of peace and not of evil, to give you a future and a hope" (Jeremiah 29:11 NKJV).

Today I am living a redeemed life with my godly husband and two grown daughters. I am rejoicing in His provision as He prepares the path before me.

I've discovered the best way to heal a broken heart is to give God all the pieces.

~ Living Truth

He heals the brokenhearted and binds up their wounds. (Psalm 147:3 NKJV)

~ Living Prayer

You are my Savior, my hope, and my deliverer. I know You will never leave me or forsake me. My orphan heart has been transformed into an adopted heart. I rest in the truth that I am my Father's beloved. I am dependent on You, Jesus, just as You are dependent on Your Heavenly Father. I am grateful for the desire in my heart to follow You. You are the God of all comfort. Thank You for using my painful experiences to minister to the lives of other broken people.

⤳ Living Action

- Are you willing to surrender embedded memories of sorrow in exchange for the hope and healing God desires to give you?
- Will you let go of unresolved hurt and let the Lord cleanse your heart toward the ones who hurt you?
- God is called the "God of hope." Will you develop a strong and confident expectation that what God promised in His Word is true? Expect great things from God; *accept* great things from God.

_____

_____

_____

_____

_____

_____

_____

_____

_____

_____

Maureen Hager is an author, inspirational speaker, and blogger. Her book, *Love's Bullet,* recounts her misguided search for love and acceptance that lured her into the life of an outlaw biker gang. Her testimony of hope and healing shows the depth of God's redemptive love for those who seek Him. You can find her at maureenhager.com and on social media at @maureen hager.

Chapter Sixteen

Building Fairytale Castles
Teresa Janzen

When my son-in-law Rick flaunted his temper as a sign of his manliness, he resembled a child throwing a tantrum to get his way. I watched as Kelly, my third daughter, learned to defuse the more public displays of his masculinity. Often she just avoided the inevitable scene by letting him opt out of family gatherings and events.

Kelly assured me, "He's all talk and steam." I believed her; well, more likely, I wanted to believer her. I hoped we had the kind of relationship where she could tell me anything, though I knew it wasn't true. Deep down, I was worried about how her state of affairs would reflect on me and my reputation in ministry and the church.

Kelly said Rick was the love of her life and described a fairytale romance. You know the kind. Girl sees boy playing horseshoes in neighbor's yard. Boy smiles and waves at girl. That was more than two years before. I could see what she saw in him. He was tall, handsome, and personable. He and his buddies roared around town on motorcycles. Perched on the back of his bike, Kelly looked like a princess being carried away by her Prince Charming. Kelly worked at a local supermarket deli, and struggled to make ends meet, while Rick stayed at home with their young son.

> Deep down, I was worried about how her state of affairs would reflect on me and my reputation in ministry and the church.

Too early one morning, the doorbell rang. Through the porch window I saw a uniformed man shifting from one foot to the other and looking up and down the street as he waited. I stared at the emblem on his sleeve—Public Safety. His head cocked to one side, he spoke into the microphone clipped to his shoulder. We locked eyes for a moment as I opened the door. "May I help you?" I asked.

The radio squawked as he released the mic. "Are you Kelly's mother?"

My identity confirmed, he said, "I need you to come down to the station and pick up your grandson."

For a moment I couldn't breathe. "What happened?" I asked.

"Everything is okay, but we need you to come right away."

Several uniformed officers were gathered in the lobby of the small-town police station when I arrived. Stepping past them, I gave the officer behind the reception desk my name and told him I was asked to come and pick up my grandson. "Are Kelly and Rick okay?" I asked. All sorts of thoughts had gone through my head on the way to the station.

The crowded room fell silent. I followed his eyes as he turned toward a bank of windows on the other side of the lobby. There was Kelly, pacing inside a small room and jostling her eighteen-month-old son to comfort him. Even from a distance I could see the bruising around her nose and eyes.

"Kelly is fine," the officer responded, "but Rick is dead."

My knees buckled. Two nearby officers grabbed my arms as I staggered backward and sank into a chair. Shades of red and black swirled before my eyes. The officer's voice echoed in my head. *What was he saying?* I forced myself to focus.

"At this point we aren't charging her," he explained. "It appears to have been self-defense."

After buckling my grandson into his car seat, I turned to my daughter. A police officer waited nearby as the two of us just held each other in the police parking lot and wept. I closed my eyes and tried to imagine this was all a dream. Kelly rested her swollen face gently against my head as she sagged into my arms like she used to when she was a little girl. She had grown so tall in these last few years, but her body now felt thin and frail.

In those moments, my emotions shifted from shock, disbelief, anger, grief, guilt, to fear. The one thing I couldn't find at that moment was hope.

I would have done anything to spare my daughter the heartache and suffering she has experienced—first as a victim and subsequently as a survivor. But releasing adult children into the world is a necessary and treacherous venture. Reflecting on my own life, I know the most difficult and heart-wrenching moments have pressed me forward—maturing and strengthening my faith. Wouldn't God do the same for my daughter? As I processed the stark reality of the situation, I was confronted with doubts and fear. Do I really trust God with the life of my daughter?

I wrestled with guilt for any part I may have inadvertently played in my daughter remaining so long in an abusive relationship. The Enemy would like nothing more than to convict me of guilt and shame. The one time Kelly had tried to escape, she called me on a stranger's phone from a restaurant parking lot after having run barefoot out of the house. That afternoon we sat on the bed she had slept in as a child, and I told her she could stay as long as she needed. She still didn't reveal everything that had been going on. After a few phone calls, Rick was at the door to pick her up. Now I wondered what I should have done that day to make her stay.

Statistics on domestic violence reveal that Kelly's response, and mine, are the norm. When family and friends attempt to intervene, abused women are often gripped with a fear of isolation, financial struggle, single parenting, or violent retribution from the perpetrator. They assure their loved ones that all is well, and they return to their abuser.

For the next few months after Rick's death, small-town gossip raged through the streets, supermarkets, and churches as people speculated about what drove this apparently happy young couple to such an end. We learned to dodge the media as we waited for the conclusion

> Reflecting on my own life, I know the most difficult and heart-wrenching moments have pressed me forward—maturing and strengthening my faith. Wouldn't God do the same for my daughter?

of the six-month investigation that informed us Kelly would not be charged in the shooting death of her boyfriend—the father of her child.

During that time of waiting, I learned to reject Satan's lies and surrender Kelly into God's hands—allowing Him to work with her through her pain. Her response in the days and months to come were her own—not mine. I knew Kelly's healing must come from her relationship with her Creator, not her mother. Surrendering her to God enabled me to find hope for the future and begin the healing process myself. Only then could God use me to minister to Kelly as she began her own journey.

Abusive relationships are a painful fact—both inside and outside the church. Some may wonder why God didn't intervene on Kelly's behalf. How could a good God allow such suffering and injustice?

God's timing is often a mystery to us. The Israelites begged God for intervention and justice as they suffered years of oppression under Pharaoh's narcissistic reign. Vacillating between reward and punishment, mercy and cruelty, Pharaoh demonstrated the classic cycle of abuse. The Israelites responded to God's intervention just as many victims respond—with relief followed by grief, then fear and a desire to return to their former situation.

Abuse is neither an event nor a cause-effect relationship—no matter if the type of oppression is physical, spiritual, sexual, verbal, or mental. Abuse is a cycle of behavior by a perpetrator toward another. It's not going to stop without some kind of intervention: intensive counseling, genuine spiritual transformation, legal action, or sometimes the tragic death of either the victim or the perpetrator.

God longs for restoration in relationships. This requires complete repentance—a change of heart and behavior. Abusers often show remorse, but that is not the same as the pride-crushing repentance that must occur before the miraculous process of transformation can begin. Make no mistake, the transformation needed for both abuser and victim is miraculous indeed.

Consider the setbacks and attitude adjustments needed to bring the children of Israel to the promised land.

> I learned to reject Satan's lies and surrender Kelly into God's hands.

They endured years of wandering, rebelling, and repenting. Pharaoh never did repent, and his pride led to destruction.

God's design for humankind is community that builds, not destroys. In Paul's first letter to the church at Corinth, he admonished the church for divisive behavior. Paul said the church is to work in community to build, but each person builds with his or her own materials (1 Corinthians 3:12). Some materials are good and will withstand judgment, but other building materials are not good and will be burned up. How we interact with one another reveals the building materials used. And what is it we are building? "Don't you realize that all of you together are the temple of God and that the Spirit of God lives in you? God will destroy anyone who destroys this temple. For God's temple is holy, and you are that temple" (1 Corinthians 3:16–17 NLT).

God's heart broke for Kelly every day she lived in fear and suffering because His love for her is even greater than mine. I may not have known everything she was going through in her relationship, but God did. His plan for Kelly included complete restoration—physical, emotional, and spiritual—and many people would be involved in that rebuilding process.

Paul reminded us that the foundation on which we build is Christ (1 Corinthians 3:11). When our children are young we teach them to build, but when they are grown they must choose their own building materials and build for themselves. As much as we want to protect and help, only God can fill their needs. When we surrender the situation into God's hands, we become an instrument He can use in the process of intervention, rescue, healing, and restoration.

> Make no mistake, the transformation needed for both abuser and victim is miraculous indeed.

Living Truth

Because of God's grace to me, I have laid the foundation like an expert builder. Now others are building on it. But whoever is building on this foundation must be very careful. For no one can lay any foundation other than the one we already have—Jesus Christ. (1 Corinthians 3:10–11 NLT)

Living Prayer

Almighty God, there are situations in life that are beyond me. Help me to surrender my loved ones to You. Where I have tried to take control, I give You control. I trust You to work these circumstances to Your good purpose and to Your glory, just as You have done so many times before. You are the only foundation on which I can build. Forgive me when I have spoken words that tear down. Please Lord, give me the right materials to build up those around me who are hurting. For those who live in fear and shame, bring hope and truth. I trust You, Lord, to bring justice in Your time. Give me strength in this season. May Your name be glorified and praised.

When our children are young we teach them to build, but when they are grown they must choose their own building materials and build for themselves.

Living Action

- Do your words and actions build up or tear down?
- When and how has God worked in your life in the midst of suffering?
- Can you choose to trust God to work in the life of your loved ones as He does in yours?

_____

_____

_____

_____

_____

_____

_____

_____

_____

_____

_____

_____

_____

_____

Author, speaker, teacher, and African explorer, Teresa Janzen invites you to thoughtful dialogue on serious topics. Bridging cultures and continents, Teresa and her husband Dan serve as missionaries in South Sudan. Teresa and her daughter are co-writing Kelly's true story of survival and journey to healing. Get updates on this and other works at teresajanzen.com.

Chapter Seventeen

Breaking Up with My Fear

Phylis Mantelli

"You can't do anything right! Why do you do this to me?" my mother screamed in my face. She wanted me to understand her point of view once again. I could never live up to her impossible standards.

The reasons behind that were much more complicated than a just a difficult relationship between a mother and daughter. My mother was mentally unstable and suffered from deep depression, anxiety, and suspected bipolar. She would spend days in bed crying and feeling the world was against her. On other days she'd tell us children she had met someone new, was getting the perfect job, everything would be excellent, and our life was about to change. But by the next day she would be disappointed by bad news or a broken promise.

She would fervently pray over her rosary beads, then read her horoscope for more direction. Her morals and ethics were so doubleminded it played into her mindset of confusion.

We were raised as Catholics. We went to church on Sundays, but never read the Bible at home. A beautiful huge Bible sat on a shelf filled with knickknacks. We rarely prayed on a consistent basis; it was only when my mom wanted something.

I was the typical rebellious teen— eager to try anything that could take me to another place so I didn't have to deal with my home life.

When we got older, my mother would go out on a Saturday night, then tell me and my siblings to go to church without her on Sunday morning. She needed alone time so she could mend her hangover.

Since I was a little girl, I felt the presence of God. He had chosen to speak to me in that small, still voice. But I was in a state of anxiety from trying to survive in the endless chaos, so His voice was drowned out. With my mother's daily outbursts, I was the parent in the relationship. I took care of my baby sister through my teen years and just shut down emotionally. I was the typical rebellious teen—eager to try anything that could take me to another place so I didn't have to deal with my home life. Drugs, sex, and danger became my normal.

I hated my mother during this time. In the rare moments I talked to God, I'd ask Him, "Why would you give me this uncaring, dangerous mom? You must really hate me." This was not the truth. The Enemy was filling my head with lies and fear.

How could I forgive a mother who was never there for me? Was it her fault that I was headed toward a harmful future because of her lack of parenting?

The act of forgiveness is described in *Webster's Dictionary* as "covered" or "to lift up."

Some of the synonyms that describe forgiveness are absolution, clemency, compassion, grace, and mercy. Forgiveness costs nothing. Bondage in unforgiveness costs everything. It took me many years to come to a place of understanding of my mother's mental health issues.

I lived in fear and anxiety most of the time. God knew when I was ready to forgive. It was smack dab in the middle of me becoming a mother myself. I needed the faithful love of Christ who was ultimately my true parent to take care of and protect me.

I prayed for God's protection many times as a young girl when my mother did not use sound judgment to keep us safe. He answered me by harboring me and my sister from further harm. God always showed me faithful love.

Now He was asking me to show forgiveness to a mother who did not deserve it. My heart needed to do this to let go of my own insecurities. More importantly, I needed to understand that my mother was not well and needed grace.

God gave me patience and grace to take care of my mother. Not always perfectly; but I was always present. When my anxious thoughts started creeping in, I recalled, "Cast all your anxiety on him because he cares for you" (1 Peter 5:7 NIV).

The fact is I do have mild depression and anxiety at times. It scared me to think I could become ill like my mother. But God—He was there to protect me from more harm. I am reminded I was predestined according to the plan of the one who works out everything in agreement with the purpose of his will (Ephesians 1:11).

David went into hiding when Saul was trying to kill him. He felt scared and asked God to be his strength, and God rescued him when he asked. He gave him Jonathan, a good friend, to help. Jonathan, Saul's own son, loved David like a brother.

"Saul ordered his son Jonathan and all his servants to kill David. But Saul's son Jonathan liked David very much, so he told him: 'My father Saul intends to kill you. Be on your guard in the morning and hide in a secret place and stay there. I'll go out and stand beside my father in the field where you are and talk to him about you. When I see what he says, I'll tell you'" (1 Samuel 19:1–3 HCSB).

God sent a safe and trusted person who could help David in his time of need. Jonathan helped David escape from Saul and even sent warnings to protect him. They wept and kissed as David had to leave the city. "Jonathan then said to David, 'Go in the assurance the two of us pledged in the name of the Lord when we said: The Lord will be a witness between you and me and between my offspring and your offspring forever.' Then David left, and Jonathan went in the city" (1 Samuel 20:42 HCSB).

God can do the same for you. He will protect you and send others to help you. He will send help through friends who become like family. He will bring people in your life who will help you and come beside you for support.

> How could I forgive a mother who was never there for me?

God was with me through all the troubles that my mother created, as well as the things I brought upon myself as a young adult. He helped me out of those tough spots and made me stronger in my dependence on Him.

When you feel weak, let Jesus be your strength. Have you been feeling as if the troubles of your past will continue in your future? Let God guide you and strengthen you. When the Enemy says you can never have the life you dream of, God will give you your heart's desire. It does not matter where you come from, you are worthy to live out a peaceful life.

 *Living Truth*

> God, hear my cry; pay attention to my prayer. I call to You from the ends of the earth when my heart is without strength. Lead me to a rock that is high above me, for You have been a refuge for me, a strong tower in the face of the enemy. I will live in your tent forever and take refuge under the shelter of your wings. (Psalm 61:1–4 HCSB)

I needed the faithful
love of Christ who was
ultimately my true
parent to take care of
and protect me.

～ *Living Prayer*

Abba Father, I pray for peace, joy, patience, and protection as I walk through a life that is sometimes anything but that. I pray for the Spirit to move in me to help others who have gone through the same pain. Help me through the rough patches of family discord. Help my mindset be about the present, and help me continue to do the things You have set up for me. I thank You for always whispering in that still small voice and showing me truth in Your love. I pray for a forgiveness for people who have harmed me. I ask for good and wise counsel from people I can trust. Do not let my anxious thoughts get in the way of the work You have in store for me, but give me a peace that surpasses all understanding. Thank You for Your love, Father God.

> When the Enemy says you can never have the life you dream of, God will give you your heart's desire.

⌐ Living Action

Perhaps take a walk and take a journal with you. Have an honest conversation with God today.

- What pain or secrets are still holding you back? Sit somewhere outside on this walk and write them down.
- Do you believe God can protect you? Ask Him to show you. Have Him bring good women into your life so you can be mentored.
- What do you want your life to look like in two years? Write down your dreams. Invite God into them. You might be surprised when you look back two years from now and see the journey.

_____

_____

_____

_____

_____

_____

_____

_____

_____

_____

Phylis Mantelli is the author of the book *Unmothered: Life with a Mom Who Couldn't Love Me*. She is also the co-host of "24 Carat Conversations" with Phylis and Rhonda. She is a certified coach and "mama mentor" to women who want to heal from broken mother/daughter relationships. You can find her at phylismantelli.com and on Facebook and Instagram.

Chapter Eighteen

God Is Enough
Cynthia Cavanaugh

Walking in the door with my sister and my aunt after a long flight, I saw my mother in a chair, frail and weak, wrapped in a blanket. She looked straight at me, her eyes seemingly boring into my soul. In a harsh tone, she asked me, "Why have you come? Your behavior will have consequences."

When she was upset with my sisters and me when we were young, her brown eyes seemed to turn black, and she would raise one eyebrow. Nothing had changed, and I felt like a small child being scolded just because I wanted to be near my mom—my dying mother. Several weeks before she had been diagnosed with cancer. Refusing any treatment, she had been told it wouldn't be long before she left us.

As she continued to lock her gaze on me, I replied, "Mom, I came to be near you and spend time with you."

When she didn't respond, and reeling from shock at her greeting, I stumbled into the bathroom, leaving my sister and my aunt at her side. In the safety of that small room in my parent's house, I began to weep. I cried out to God, doubting there would ever be any reconciliation with my mother and desperate for at least a scrap of acceptance from her.

> **I felt like a small child being scolded just because I wanted to be near my mom—my dying mother.**

I came because I loved her and was met with rebuke. I tried to excuse her behavior because I knew she was on pain medication, and yet it was reminiscent of many episodes of verbally abusive and hurtful words.

It was difficult watching the days go by during our visit, the house bustling with hospice nurses and friends stopping by. My dad often sat outside on the porch, sad and lonely and trying to grab as many moments with his bride as possible. Often he was swept away by caregivers and nurses as they tried to make my mom as comfortable as possible.

I longed for a few minutes to be with her alone, but since her hospital bed was set up downstairs in the family room in the center of their small A-frame home, it was next to impossible. We took turns singing to her and sitting by her side to read, but there were always others nearby.

But one day a few days before we left, the house was quiet and relatively empty. *This is my chance to talk with Mom alone*, I thought. I read her a chapter from my new book on the story of Job and suffering that was days away from being released. With tears streaming down her face, she said, "This is good, really good." And then she said, "I am so proud of you."

I knew she loved me in her way, but I also understood my mom was broken. She spent most of her childhood during the Second World War in Europe and at one point lived in a refugee camp before she emigrated with her family to the United States when she was twelve years old. She witnessed firsthand what no child should have to experience and endured trauma that left deep scars. Because of this, I had learned to accept that, for whatever reason, she was incapable of giving me what I thought I needed as a daughter. I had come to this conclusion years earlier after spending many hours in counseling and after many futile attempts to gain her love and acceptance. *Now she is finally telling me how proud she is of me?* I couldn't even respond.

"You do know I am proud of you, right?" she said when I didn't answer.

"No, Mom, I don't know."

Tears started to roll down the side of her face again as she locked eyes with me again. This time I looked into eyes filled with kindness and regret.

Through my tears, I gently said, "Mom, I forgive you."

We didn't unpack all our relational pain and frustration, but this was enough. Enough for now.

As I drove back to my friend's house where I was staying, I wept. Knowing she would soon die, I had resigned myself that there would be no resolve or acceptance from my mother this side of heaven. But God gave me this small gift on her death-bed, and I embraced her kind words. They didn't erase all the unresolved emotional abuse and manipulation over the years, but this still was a gift of grace.

Harsh words and emotional manipulation remind me of the story in Genesis 16 of Sarah and Hagar's rivalry. If you know the story, you know Sarah couldn't conceive a child. God promised her and her husband Abraham that they would have a child, but Sarah became impatient. To speed things up, she decided she would have a son through her servant Hagar, as was a barren wife's custom in ancient times. When Hagar got pregnant, Sarah complained, "She looked on me with contempt" (Genesis 16:5 ESV). Hagar flaunted her pregnancy in front of her mistress; in turn, she was harshly treated by Sarah and fled alone into the desert. God sent Hagar an angel who gave her a promise and told her she would have a son, and he would be a great man. In reply, Hagar said, "You are a God of seeing." She added, "Truly here I have seen him who looks after me" (Genesis 16:13 ESV).

When we are treated harshly by those we love and especially our parents, we can spend our whole lives looking for acceptance.

But God sees.

By definition, verbal abuse can be seen as a chronic stream of words that can wash over a person's soul and leave deep wounds and scars.

But God sees.

Abuse can leave a trail of hurt and cripple a person's ability to have a secure identity.

Because of this, I had learned to accept that, for whatever reason, she was incapable of giving me what I thought I needed as a daughter.

But God sees.

We can find ourselves like Hagar alone in the desert and running away from life.

But God sees.

Despite my mom's inability to nurture and give acceptance, she had a strong faith and was a prayer warrior. After she died, we found reams of her written prayers for her family and those she served. One consolation for me in reading her prayer journal was hearing her tender prayers for my family and me. She wasn't able to verbalize those words to us, but she could write them in a sacred space to her God.

As I shared at her memorial, I spoke openly about the oil and water relationship we had, not divulging dishonoring details. I asked God, "Lord, give me a voice to honor Mom at the service." He helped me see we are all broken, some of us more than others. My mom had a sincere faith. She sought God with all of her heart and prayed fervently. When she was alive, I never understood how she could have such a healthy prayer life and still be unable to resolve our issues.

After her death, God gave me another gift in reflection. He challenged me to focus on all the good things about Mom and the legacy she left—her love of music, baking, and serving others. She taught me to be responsible and have a heart of integrity.

But the most important gift she gave me was in leading me by example that God is enough.

No human being, no matter how close or intimate, can take the place of God in my life. She would often tell me, "God is enough for me. It doesn't matter if people don't understand me." I was always puzzled by this because I attributed it to a lack of empathy, and her stubborn refusal to resolve her relationship issues.

But it became clear in her death. My mom knew what Jesus had done for her, and it was enough. In her mind, it was either God was enough or He wasn't—there was no in between. It was a choice, and she chose to believe God is enough.

Despite all the hurt and the wrongs I could point to, I choose to remember

> She wasn't able to verbalize those words to us, but she could write them in a sacred space to her God.

this one gift she gave, and it covers the pain.

My mom knew what Jesus had done for her, and it was enough.

As my sisters and cousins sang "It Is Well With My Soul" at the end of our tribute at the memorial, those words became my solace. And despite the grief of what I wished could have happened, I am grateful God has helped me understand. In this life, there is nothing more precious and holy than the phrase, "God is enough."

 ## Living Truth

I say to myself, "The Lord is everything I will ever need. So I will put my hope in him." (Lamentations 3:24 NIRV)

Living Prayer

God, help me realize there is no one else like You. No one else can fill my soul as You do. Give me understanding, and allow me to have compassion for the brokenness I see in others, realizing that I, too, am broken and will fail in my relationships. I place all my expectations in You. You and You alone are my source of strength, refuge, and shelter when I come against the brokenness of those who have hurt me. Help me forgive and love as You call me to love.

∽ *Living Action*

- Read the full story of Hagar in Genesis 16. Picture yourself in the desert like Hagar, exhausted, weary, alone, and tired. Where does God need to be enough for you right now?
- Take some time to reflect and confess where or on whom you have misplaced your expectations.
- Where is God asking you to submit and surrender?
- Write out a prayer, confess, surrender, and tell God what you need.

_____

_____

_____

_____

_____

_____

_____

_____

_____

_____

_____

_____

Managing Editor Cynthia Cavanaugh is a speaker, life coach, and award-winning author of *Anchored: Leading through the Storms* and *Live Bold: A Devotional to Strengthen Your Soul*. She is the director of program design and development for Redemption Press, and you can find her at cynthiacavanaugh.com, Facebook, Instagram, and her new podcast, *The Soul Anchor*.

Part 4

Mental Health

Chapter Nineteen

Words That Changed My Life
Cheri Keaggy

One ordinary Sunday evening in September my sister called from California. "Where are you?" she asked. Immediately, I knew it must be serious.

Home with my husband in Tennessee, I sat up in bed to hear words that would forever alter my life.

"Dad's dead," she said. "He shot himself in the backyard."

I couldn't believe what I had just heard. Yes, my father had been sick, in and out of the hospital, and set to see a specialist the following week. Still, the news of his sudden passing came as a complete shock.

For the next several hours, I cried and rocked, rocked and cried, repeating this guttural prayer: "Please take care of my daddy tonight, Lord. Please take care of my daddy tonight." I finally climbed out of bed around 4:00 a.m. to scribble a whirl-wind of thoughts in my journal.

The mystery of Psalm 116:15 (NKJV) cut through my desperation. "Precious in the sight of the Lord is the death of His saints." I kept repeating those words over and over again.

Could it be that Dad's departure could actually be a blessing to God? In my anguish, somehow the thought comforted me.

> Could it be that
> Dad's departure could
> actually be a blessing
> to God?

As reality began to sink in the next day, I remember thinking, *You didn't have to do that, Dad. You didn't have to do that.*

After quickly breaking the news to my two adult children, I was on a plane to Mom. No point in wearing makeup; too many tears. This would be my first time flying to California when Dad wouldn't be there on the other end. As the plane took off, I turned toward the window to hide my tears and began to write a note to Dad in heaven. I wrote, "It's okay, Dad, you can be at peace now. Relish this time with Jesus."

I fingered the silver anchor charm around my neck, a gift from a friend following a retreat centered on Hebrews 6:19: "We have this hope as an anchor for the soul, firm and secure." In that moment, it brought a measure of solace. It was a reminder of all I know to be true, a reminder of our great hope—something Dad no longer has need of.

The youngest of two boys, Michael Duane Anderson was born in 1939. He was a husband, a son, an uncle, a father, a grandfather, and just four months prior to his death, he had become a great-grandpa for the first time. Physically active throughout his life, he was a Marine veteran, a retired deputy sheriff, and an accomplished rock climber having conquered Yosemite Valley's iconic Half Dome and El Capitan like a rock star. A man who felt closest to God in the great outdoors, he hiked more than fourteen thousand miles along the Pacific Crest Trail and the John Muir Trail. Many routes, many times.

Besides his unquenchable appetite for adventure, perhaps this was, in part, a quest for peace from inner conflict. Though never entangled in drug or alcohol addiction, it seems my father never experienced the healing he sought from the wounds of a tumultuous childhood.

Throughout his life, Dad struggled with anger and rage. Though never officially diagnosed, one counselor suspected PTSD, while his near obsession with order likely pointed to OCD. Could this have been an attempt to control his surroundings as things felt so out of control in his family of origin? Perhaps. He certainly was searching, reading countless self-help books while faithfully recording episodes of Dr. Phil.

A love of music surely brought both joy and escape as he was a skilled accordion player and had amassed an impressive collection of operas, symphonies, and classical music. He rarely missed my piano recitals and was one of my biggest fans from day one. For this, and so many other reasons, I am grateful.

Still, Dad was a bit of a loner. Though a sincere believer, he had a more private expression of faith. Instead of being baptized during a regular service at my childhood church, I can remember returning after everyone had gone home so Dad could be baptized with just the pastor and our family present. Even so, he diligently studied the Bible and Christian theology. In fact, I was tickled to learn that he used to "smuggle" torn-out pages of Scripture into work at the L.A. County Jail. He was hungry for God's Word. The thought brings tears to my eyes even now.

I'm no expert on mental health and couldn't begin to conjecture all the reasons behind my father's decision to take his life that day. Was it depression, exhaustion, fear, despair due to his failing health? Or perhaps was it the negative side effects of pain meds from the hospital? We may never know this side of heaven.

But I proclaim as the apostle Paul did from his prison cell, "To live is Christ, and to die is gain" (Philippians 1:21 NKJV). I believe with all my heart that Dad's final cry for mercy did not fall on deaf ears. He knew where he was going, for he had believed on the name of Jesus. Because of Christ's death and resurrection, he would be absent from the body, present with the Lord (2 Corinthians 5:8).

As believers, we grieve though not as those without hope (1 Thessalonians 4:13). Still, I cannot emphasize enough the suffering my father's choice caused. While he may have ended his own pain, he multiplied it exponentially for all who loved him.

In the book *Aftershock: Help, Hope, and Healing in the Wake of Suicide,*[2] the authors said, "Every suicide survivor is looking for a way to feel normal again following a life event that is so abnormal."

It has taken me awhile. Songwriting has helped me process some of my emotions:

It seems my father never experienced the healing he sought from the wounds of a tumultuous childhood.

You left a note for mother, but there was none for me.
If I didn't know how much you cared, guess I'd still be angry.
The power of a moment. You just can't take it back.
Lord, have mercy for the things we lack.[3]

I never thought suicide would be a part of my story. This grief and its impact has surprised me like no other. And yet, my Bible tells me, "Blessed are those who mourn for they will be comforted" (Matthew 5:4 NIV).

In God's matchless mercy, that is exactly what He has done. Under the guidance of a grief counselor, my Wonderful Counselor brought specific healing through the writing of a completion letter. I was able to say all the things I didn't get to say to Dad before he died. Our relationship is eternal, not just as father and daughter, but as brother and sister in Christ. This is a temporary "goodbye" and a hope-filled "see you later" all at the same time. I am so grateful for that perspective.

In his book *Grieving a Suicide: A Loved One's Search for Comfort, Answers, and Hope,* Albert Y. Hsu wrote, "Grief that has done its work in us will help us experience God's grace more fully."[4]

I have found that to be true. "Though He brings grief, He will show compassion, so great is his unfailing love" (Lamentations 3:32 NIV).

It is often said the depth of one's grief speaks to the significance of the relationship. This has been a significant grief. But it is a grief held safely in the loving arms of Jesus—the Living Hope who brings hope to the living.

```
While he may have
ended his own pain,
he multiplied it
exponentially for all
who loved him.
```

～ Living Truth

I have set before you life and death . . . now choose life. (Deuteronomy 30:19 NIV)

"Grief that has done its work in us will help us experience God's grace more fully."

～ Living Prayer

Lord, thank You for the gift of life. Help me to receive the abundant life You intend for me, and empower me to speak words of life to others.

～ Living Action

One statistic reveals that every seventeen minutes, someone, somewhere, chooses death.

- Are you struggling with depression or suicidal thoughts? I am here to tell you, you're not alone. Though you may feel hopeless, you don't have to take an irreversible action right now. There are other options. You were born for a purpose and are dearly loved. You may think the world would be better without you in it. Trust me. There could be nothing further from the truth. There are many who would be devastated if you were not here. Life might seem unbearable now, but God sees you and has a hope and future for you. Will you reach out for help?

- Call the National Suicide Prevention Lifeline: 1-800-273-TALK (1-800-273-8255). If the call doesn't go through, try again. Or phone a trusted friend, pastor, or family member.
- Do you know someone who may be suffering from suicidal thoughts? Studies show that asking if they've battled suicidal thoughts, or if they have ever considered how they might carry it out, can actually bring relief. God may want to use you to open the door for conversation and an opportunity to offer help, resources, and friendship.

_____

_____

_____

_____

_____

_____

_____

_____

_____

_____

_____

_____

With over twenty-five years' ministry experience, Cheri has released nine albums garnering nine number one songs, three Dove Award nominations, and a Dove Award win. A prolific songwriter, speaker, blogger, and published author, Cheri lives with her husband in Tennessee and has two adult children and one grandchild. Connect with her at cherikeaggy.com, @CheriKeaggy, and ckeaggybooking@gmail.com.

Chapter Twenty

What I Found Knee-Deep in a Mess
Carole Leathem

"Why is this happening?" I asked as I walked out of the hospital alone, terrified, and angry early that Thursday morning. As the doors closed slowly behind me, I started screaming the question in the dark parking lot.

An armed guard had escorted me out of the psychiatric emergency room. "Don't come back," he said. "They will call you when he gets settled into a secure facility."

My pastor husband of forty years had been placed on a seventy-two-hour psychiatric hold. I had heard jokes about being "5150ed," and I had just learned what that code meant. He was now a ward of the State of California, and I had no say in the matter.

As I drove home, I continued to ask, "Why is this happening?" over and over. I fell asleep asking the question, dreamed it, and found the words waiting for me when I woke up. The next morning, sitting on the sofa at my son's house, with a cup of coffee and my Bible, I continued to ask, "Why is this happening?"

I had made a commitment to watch CJ, my two-year-old grandson who was still asleep, and everyone else was gone. Several times I walked down the hall to the bedroom. Each time I opened the door I hoped I would find my husband sleeping in the bed. But the room was still empty.

> There is no way I would ever consider my husband's anxiety, depression, and suicidal thoughts a sheer gift.

I was awake, but in the middle of a nightmare. My life had fallen apart, and I had no idea what to do. Laying my head on the arm of the sofa, I turned to God and began to pray. My heart felt like it was going to explode. Through my tears, I begged God to answer my question.

When I closed my eyes, I heard God say to me, *You have to trust me, Carole. This is going to be hard, and it will get worse. I love you, baby girl, and I will carry you when you can't go on. Read James. I have a message for you.*

With excitement, I turned in my Bible to James to see what the message might be. I began to read the words out loud. James 1:2 in *The Message* says, "Consider it a sheer gift, when tests and challenges come at you from all sides." I slammed the book down on the cushion and yelled, "Really, God? A gift? Thanks, but no thanks!" There is no way I would ever consider my husband's anxiety, depression, and suicidal thoughts a sheer gift. I opened up the Bible app on my phone and looked up the verse in the New International Version. This time it said, "Consider it pure joy, my brothers and sisters, whenever you face trials of many kinds." This was worse, a sheer gift, and now pure joy?

I yelled out loud into the empty room, "God, are You clueless? Are You aware of what happened last night?" I imagine God was smiling at me as I ranted on and on because He knew; He was there.

We are now five years into my husband's struggle with mental illness and have experienced so much chaos, pain, and fear. We still have no medical answers, but the depression and suicidal thoughts are under control for the moment with medication. My husband struggles with anxiety daily.

Early on, I stopped asking God, "Why is this happening?" I began to say, "Okay God, this is happening, now what do I do?" The change of questions opened my eyes to the many ways God prepared my life in advance of what we now refer to as "The Crash." I can also see God at work every day providing and taking care of us.

The message God wanted me to find in James has become a truth I cling to every moment of my journey. I try to read other Scriptures, but I keep returning to the first five verses of James 1. As the message became more transparent, my fear of the trials became the anticipation of the journey, and I have found joy. I was knee-deep in a mess, and the joy started flowing. Sometimes a messy life requires a concentrated look at a portion of Scripture. Sometimes that is all you can handle.

The truths God wanted me to find in James 1:2–5 are these:

A New Perspective on Trials

God sees trials differently than we do. We see trials as something terrible happening to us. God sees them as a way to develop a deeper level of trust and faith in Him. When trials come, we can let fear and anger control us, or we can choose to trust God. When I choose to trust God, I am choosing joy. I can have joy when life is messy and painful because my joy comes from the relationship I have with God, not in the circumstances.

Brace or Lean

God says, "when" not if trials come. He tells us that trials will come, and when they show up, we can do one of two things. We can brace against the trial or lean into God. When we brace against the trial, we are taking control and trying to fix things. When we lean into God, we are giving the responsibility to God and trusting Him. It was never my job to fix my husband and find a solution to his mental illness. My job was to love my husband and trust God.

The Fear Factor

God has a plan to use the trials for our growth. I have learned to live *with* fear, not *in* fear. My fears are real: What if the medication stops working? What if the depression and suicidal thoughts

> Sometimes a messy life requires a concentrated look at a portion of Scripture. Sometimes that is all you can handle.

come back? My husband has mental illness; what will people think? How will I pay all the medical bills?

When I get caught up in these fears, I start taking charge. I am trying to control past and present circumstances that are out of my control. This action drains my energy, and I become angry and afraid all over again. Living *with* fear means I understand God has designed fear for several purposes.

Fear can be a protector and will warn us that we are in danger. That danger can be physical or emotional. Fear creates the need for action, to move to safety to protect me. Most of the time, fear says, "Don't just stand there. Do something."

Fear as a motivator says, "Don't just do something, stand there." Motivating fear causes me to take a deep breath, pay attention, and ask the right questions.

When my husband was placed in the psychiatric hospital, I started asking the wrong question, "Why is this happening?" When I began saying, "Okay, God, this is happening, now what?" my focus changed from living in fear to trusting God and living with the fear.

Ask Boldly

God wants us to turn to Him and ask boldly for help when the trials come. My bold ask has become, "God show me what to do!" Sometimes I admit I get sarcastic and say, "Okay, how are You going to fix this one, God?" Either way, I am boldly expecting God to show up. I am telling God the truth about how I feel and asking for His help. Most of the time when I ask, the answer is already there waiting for me.

It was never my job to
fix my husband and
find a solution to his
mental illness. My job
was to love my husband
and trust God.

~ *Living Truth*

Consider it a sheer gift, friends, when tests and challenges come at you from all sides. You know that under pressure, your faith-life is forced into the open and shows its true colors. So, don't try to get out of anything prematurely. Let it do its work, so you become mature and well-developed, not deficient in any way. If you don't know what you're doing, pray to the Father. He loves to help. You'll get His help and won't be condescended to when you ask for it. Ask boldly, believingly, without a second thought. (James 1:2–5 MSG)

When I began saying, "Okay, God, this is happening, now what?" my focus changed from living in fear to trusting God and living with the fear.

~ *Living Prayer*

God, I am choosing to trust You. I am so afraid, and I don't know what to do. I am choosing to lean into You for comfort, peace, and direction. I give You this trial in my hands. Please take it. I know You have a plan, and I trust You to take care of me, hold me, love me, and guide me. I choose joy because I belong to You.

⤳ *Living Action*

- Name the trial you are going through.
- Are you willing to be truthful with God about how you feel?
- Do you find yourself living *in* fear instead of *with* fear?
- Can you ask God boldly for what you need? Right now, cup your hands and imagine putting the trial in your palms. Lift your hands to God and pray the above prayer.

_____

_____

_____

_____

_____

_____

_____

_____

_____

_____

_____

_____

Carole Leathem is an encouraging storyteller and speaker. She loves God, and this gives her the strength to be transparent. She lives every day with joy and will boldly tell you about her messy life and show you how God continues to show up. Visit Carole at carolesjourney.com.

Chapter Twenty-One

Brutiful Love and Truth
Margaret Molloy

I awakened at 2:00 a.m. unable to return to my fitful sleep, knowing I needed to drive the hour to see my brother Matt. I had made this trip so many times before. Previous visits had been infused with anger, fear, compassion, and enabling. Looping through my mind was the thought, *What will I find this time?*

Relieved to see him alive, I told him, "I have no agenda." I was just there because God woke me up and compelled me to come. "I don't want you to die alone," I said.

He assured me as only an addict can, "I am not going to die."

As we talked through the night, this time it was different. He started facing the painful wounding in his past. He was climbing out of the pit. In the wee hours of the morning, he prayed the most honest, humble, poignant prayer I have ever heard. It was a "good relapse."

He returned to treatment.

A few weeks later, I was penning his eulogy.

Penning my younger brother's eulogy was a "brutiful" experience. Brutal. Beautiful. He was only fifty-one years old, his slow suicide the effect of his addiction to alcohol.

Jonah and Whale Rehab

When I think of the interactions between an addict and his or her loved ones, it reminds me of the biblical prophet Jonah.

God told Jonah to go to the city of Nineveh and warn the people He was displeased with them. Jonah did not want to go, so he ran away in the opposite direction, ultimately boarding a ship to escape from God's purpose.

Suddenly terrible winds blew and the ship was in danger of splitting apart. Terrified sailors called out to their gods to no avail. Next they threw cargo off in hopes the ship would stabilize. Still the storm raged on. The captain, exasperated with Jonah, ordered him to call out to his God to stop the storm. And where was Jonah while chaos abounded? Below deck, sound asleep while everyone around him risked their livelihoods, even their very lives, dealing with a storm spawned by his disobedience.

Figuring the storm was Jonah's fault, they questioned him, and he confessed who he was and that he was running away from his God: "the God of heaven, who made the sea and the dry land" (Jonah 1:9 NIV). This terrified them even further. The storm worsened. They asked Jonah what they should do to make it stop. He told them to throw him overboard. I imagine the sailors argued as the Bible tells us they wanted to enable Jonah, to row him to shore rather than turn him over to God. But they eventually threw him overboard, and Jonah went to "whale rehab."

God purposes for addicts to be free, yet like Jonah, they often run for the opposite. Then many who love the addict try to row them to shore so they don't find themselves in the belly of a whale, terrified and alone, with life slipping away. We sacrifice our own resources and relationships instead of letting the addict realize his need to be in God's hands alone.

I finally understood that to love my brother *brutifully*, I had to throw him overboard. No lifejacket.

In Jonah 2, we get a glimpse into Jonah's rehab journal. He fought his demons of lies—the crippling lies that

> When I think of the interactions between an addict and his or her loved ones, it reminds me of the biblical prophet Jonah.

he had been abandoned by and banished from God. While his life ebbed away, he recognized the futility of clinging to worthless idols. And then, turning toward the living hope, Jonah shouted with grateful praise, "Salvation comes from the Lord!"

God purposes for addicts to be free, yet like Jonah, they often run for the opposite.

That's what Matt's early morning prayer that day sounded like. He knew his salvation came from the Lord.

Although I don't identify as much with Jonah's addict-like behaviors, I do relate to post-whale-rehab Jonah. He was biased against the gentile Ninevites, thinking them to be a threat to Israel's peace and economic stability. After he righted his heart with God while in the whale, Jonah preached to the Ninevites. Like the Grinch awaiting Whoville to wake up to a present-less Christmas morning, Jonah perched himself on the sky-view box awaiting the Ninevites' destruction. Much to Jonah's chagrin, the Ninevites repented. You would think Jonah would be happy for them, but he was not. He was angry they weren't going to get wiped off the earth after all. I imagine his bizarre prayer letter might have read:

> Dear Supporters,
>
> I wish you all hadn't prayed so much for the revival. Unfortunately, they all repented; 120,000 souls were saved. God was merciful. I'm depressed.
>
> Bitterly Yours,
> Jonah.

I see myself in Jonah though. God sent me to a people who I loved very much, until they wronged me or mine.

My family ventured to a simple resort for vacation every year. One night, we went out to dinner at a local restaurant. The owner opened his home to us for an evening of fun. The owner's son was the same age as my middle son, and they

We sacrifice our own resources and relationships instead of letting the addict realize his need to be in God's hands alone.

played on their Game Boys together while the rest of us danced to the oldies. When it was time to go, we couldn't find our son's Game Boy.

Like Jonah, bigotry captured my heart. *These people are prone to steal. I bet that boy stole my son's Game Boy.* I insisted on searching the house they had so hospitably invited us into. Even now as I recall my horrific behavior, I cringe.

God's question to Jonah concerning the plant could be asked of me, "Margaret, do you care more about a toy than you do for people living in spiritual darkness?" I cared more about a toy than about the precious souls of our hosts.

When we returned to the resort, I found my son's Game Boy. It had been there all along. We went back right away to apologize, but the damage had been done. I still pray for that family, that despite my awful witness, they would find salvation that comes from the Lord Jesus.

There is brutiful love in that experience too. The brutal truth is that I am among the worst of sinners *and* God will still use me to reveal His beautiful plan of salvation to others. Brutiful. Brutal. Beautiful.

At Matt's service, I concluded his eulogy with these words.

> In a few minutes we will sing our song of farewell, "You Are Mine" by David Haas. The lyrics help us worship the I Am. The I Am who says He is the Way, the Truth, and the Life. The last stanza gives us the strength to say farewell. In Matt's final seconds on earth,

he stopped breathing, and his physical body fell to the ground. But I Am was there. We take comfort knowing that in those seconds, Jesus, I Am, called Matt's name, embraced his pain and said, "Stand up now, walk and live."

Living Truth

But because of His great love for us, God, who is rich in mercy, made us alive with Christ even when we were dead in transgressions—it is by grace you have been saved. (Ephesians 2:4–5 NIV)

Living Prayer

We praise and thank You because You are rich in mercy. We repent from trying to be You in others' lives, not willing for them to suffer. Help us to "throw them overboard" so they can turn away from idols and turn toward You. You and You alone are our salvation. Even when we are dead in our sins, Your great love for us calls us to repentance as we put our hope in You and are saved. Help us to love our neighbors, each and every one of them, as You do, Lord. Thank You for saving us by grace.

I cared more about a toy than about the precious souls of our hosts.

～ *Living Action*

- Is there someone you love who needs to be "thrown overboard" so he or she can cry out to God and be saved?
- Jonah struggled to love those he was biased against. Is there someone you have bias against, someone who you think deserves punishment but instead life has gone well for?

_____

_____

_____

_____

_____

_____

_____

_____

_____

_____

_____

_____

Margaret Molloy is also known by her pen name Marmi B. Molloy. She lived and labored in Indonesia for eleven years, and Marmi is her Indonesian name. B is for Brown, her last name during her twenty-seven-year marriage; Molloy is her maiden name. She has three amazing adult children.

Chapter Twenty-Two

Understanding My Emotions
Faye Sant'Anna

When the phone rang around 8:00 p.m., the caller ID said Wishard Hospital in Indianapolis. I immediately knew who would be on the other line.

"Hello?" I said as I heard an intense cry. It was my mom, and she was very upset.

"Get me out of here! I don't belong here. If I have to stay here, I'm going to die!" She kept saying these words over and over.

"Mom, at this time, you need to stay there. You are not going to die. On the contrary, you are going to feel better." Then I hung up, heartbroken. I cried out to God and asked Him to visit my mom and to give her peace.

Two years before that phone call, I had visited my dad in a psychiatric hospital in Boston where he had been admitted for eight days with the diagnosis of chronic depression. He could not stop crying, and when the situation escalated quickly, his psychiatrist felt it was best for him to be admitted.

Now it was my mother's turn.

I had told my mother's doctor if she didn't admit her, I would be her next patient because of all the stress I was under watching my mother lose her mind. My mom had a psychotic breakdown, and the best way for her to be treated was in a hospital with a team of doctors who could evaluate her and try the best treatments

Mom and Dad were expected to be perfect and to lead people by example.

for her. The diagnosis she received was manic bipolar disorder.

How did we end up here?

My dad had been a Southern Baptist pastor for over thirty years when all of this started. My mom was dedicated to serving the church and specifically the children's ministry. Mom and Dad were expected to be perfect and to lead people by example.

How did such firm believers end up in a psychiatric hospital? The shame of having to let people know what was happening, canceling church, and calling their workplaces, was overwhelming.

Very quickly the shame and guilt crept into my mind. I thought, *Your whole family is a disgrace to the church of Christ!*

But why? Why are shame and guilt the first feelings to surface when a psychiatric issue comes up? Society wants to label psychiatric patients as crazy and untrustworthy. I have discovered that, unfortunately, people are often just not educated enough on mental health issues.

Mental health has been discussed and exposed for thousands of years. Open your Bible and you will see many people who suffered anxiety, panic attacks, depression, and other mental breakdowns. From the Old to the New Testament, the Bible exposes multiple stories of mental health issues.

One of the most fascinating of these characters in the Bible is King David. His life was a constant roller coaster, filled with ups and downs and twists and turns. From a humble shepherd boy to fighting a giant, playing music for the king, and then becoming the king, he was loved and hated. He held his newborn son, and then he buried him. There were times of war and times of peace.

He experienced way more than any one of us could handle. But what I love most about David is the way he was open about his emotions and exposed his feelings about everything. He never hid what he was feeling from God. God called David a man after His own heart. Amazing!

In Psalm 13:2–3 (csb), David lamented, "How long will I store up anxious concerns within me, agony in my mind every day? How long will my enemy dominate me? Consider me and answer, Lord my God. Restore brightness to my eyes; otherwise, I will sleep in death."

In the Bible we read that often when David prayed, he turned depression into praise, but he was always open about his emotions. In Psalm 102:4 (CSB), David also talked to God about his heart, "My heart is suffering, withered like grass; I even forget to eat my food."

Of course, there were no mental health specialists back then in Jerusalem and no access to the wide range of antidepressants we have today. David just did what he knew—he prayed. He cried out to God. He exposed his emotions. He shared his emotions. He opened his heart. He did not ignore his feelings, but instead talked to God and asked Him for help. And then he often sought out the prophet Nathan and Samuel for counsel. He rarely ever isolated himself.

How about you? What are you doing to take care of your emotions? Would you take a deep breath today and look into your heart? Would you examine how everything is inside your mind? What do you need to do to feel better? Do you need to re-evaluate your relationships? Put your priorities in order? Do you need to seek help from a professional? Do you need a chemical balance analysis? There are so many questions and so many answers that need to be addressed. Can you stop and address them today?

"For who knows a person's thoughts except his spirit within him?" (1 Corinthians 2:11 CSB). You are the only one who can take inventory of your life. Mental health is just as important as seeking out a cardiologist or the ER if you are having sharp pain in your chest. We don't hesitate to address symptoms of a heart attack, but we will often ignore the symptoms in our mind and soul. Check your emotions and please do it today.

Don't wait until you have to be taken to a psychiatric hospital to be analyzed like my parents were. I am thankful for the medical professionals who helped both my parents in two different cities and two different hospitals. They literally saved their lives! But I also often wonder how different this situation would have been if they had taken care of their emotions

From the Old to the New Testament, the Bible exposes multiple stories of mental health issues.

from the beginning and had adhered to the warning signs. It is likely they probably would not have gone through the traumatic experience of being admitted.

Jesus sees the depths of our hearts and He does not leave us like we are. He heals and restores. He places the right people around us to help. Today, I am the person reminding you to look into your heart and soul. Take care of yourself. There is no shame or guilt in doing so. You are important. You are needed, you matter, and you are loved.

Philippians 4:6 (NLT) says, "Do not be anxious about anything, but in every situation, by prayer and petition, with thanksgiving, present your requests to God."

If just thinking about getting help causes your anxiety level to increase, stop and ask God to show you the right professional you should talk to. Do your research and look for help. There are amazing medical professionals available to help you. Do it today.

After leaving the hospital, both my parents continued with medication they are still using over fifteen years later. The medicines have helped them to balance the brain, and therapy helped them both deal with their emotions. Counseling has helped them learn how to deal with life situations that come to rob our joy and peace. We no longer have guilt or shame when talking about their mental health. Their marriage has been restored and their health is well balanced. They are finally happy.

There is hope and help available to you also.

In Psalm 108 (CSB), David spoke about his heart on that day after being restored: "My heart is confident, God; I will sing; I will sing praises."

When we share our feelings and seek help, we will receive it and can find happiness again.

Today, I am the person
reminding you to look
into your heart and
soul.

Living Truth

For who knows a person's thoughts except his spirit within him? (1 Corinthians 2:11 csb)

When we share our feelings and seek help, we will receive it and can find happiness again.

Living Prayer

Jesus, I want to bring before You all my emotions, my feelings, and my soul. I ask You to give me joy today. I ask You to show me if I need to seek professional help. If I do, give me the courage to do so, and show me the best way to find help. Place the right people to help me in this journey. I have tasted and seen that You are good, and I know it is Your desire for me to be whole. You died to give me life and life in abundance. I want to live the best life with You, Jesus. I thank You for caring enough for my whole being.

⟶ *Living Action*

- What is the first step this week you can take to feel better emotionally?
- What changes need to happen so you can identify how your emotions are?

_____

_____

_____

_____

_____

_____

_____

_____

_____

_____

_____

_____

_____

_____

Faye Sant'Anna is originally from Brazil and currently resides in Indianapolis, Indiana, with her husband Glenn, two children Matthew and Julia, and their dog Harley. Faye is very active in her church and the Indianapolis community. She is also the founder and CEO of the Miracle Barn & Unusual Love Ministries.

Chapter Twenty-Three

My Mother's Daughter
Denise Ann Goosby

I COULD HEAR MY MOTHER'S VOICE BEHIND ME. It began as a rough whisper, barely discernible amid the din of the store. Then it grew a bit fiercer—angrier. I turned to look at her, and then quickly turned back and kept walking straight ahead.

Not again, I cried inwardly.

I could feel the fear and shame rising up, overwhelming my chubby, pig-tailed, child's body.

Please don't get too loud, Mom, I silently pleaded.

Of course, I couldn't tell her. Wouldn't dare tell her. I hadn't gotten a spanking in a while. And I was not about to do anything to bring on another one. But I dreaded the stares and snickers from the people around us.

"Just let us get back to the car soon," I mumbled, walking quicker to the door I saw just ahead.

I burst through it and kept on walking. Maybe I wouldn't be embarrassed this time.

"Denise Ann! Why are you walking so fast? Don't you see these cars out here?"

And people turned and stared.

That was a lot of my childhood. Whether washing dishes, watering the lawn, or walking through the store with me, my mom, Anna, would talk to herself. Sometimes she would talk to those I couldn't see—uttering words that were harsh and brutal and profane. Words that never should be spoken in earshot of a child. One of my mom's younger sister's lived next door to us, and I often escaped to her house to hide from my mom and the voices.

My aunt said my mom helped raise her and their siblings after their mother left home and their dad was left with the children. A lot of the responsibility fell to my mom. My aunt thought it was too much for her.

When my mom married at twenty-one and was ready to have children of her own, she couldn't. She miscarried several times before having me and my younger sister before turning forty. My aunt told me my mom had spent time in a special hospital.

Oh, she was like her other sister, I thought warily to myself.

This illness of the mind not only affected my mom but another sister too. She was like Mom, speaking to people who weren't there, swearing and shouting. Only worse.

I remember seeing a bunch of strangers put her in a white van and drive off. People said she was going to get some medicine that would make her feel better and be better.

Why couldn't they do the same for my mom?

As I grew, I wondered, *Will the same happen to me? Will I start to hear voices?* Would I speak to people who weren't there or make a spectacle of myself to the shame of those around me? How could I outrun my legacy? My mom, aunt, and—I later learned—my paternal grandmother all suffered from mental illness. Would I suffer the same fate?

I was tired. Tired of the isolation. Tired of not being able to have classmates over at my home. Tired of having my mom be mean to me. Tired of being worried about what other people thought of my family.

`As I grew, I wondered, Will the same happen to me? Will I start to hear voices?`

My dad, God bless him, tried to shield me from some of the madness. He was my champion and defender.

But he was hiding too. As a minister, he couldn't afford to have his ill wife and family issues exposed for his friends and colleagues and congregants to see. Like me, he kept his pain inside.

> I am my mother's daughter—but more importantly, I am my Father's daughter.

God doesn't want us to hide in our pain or fear that our future can't be good. Our destiny doesn't depend on our parentage. What my mom, aunt, and grandmother lived did not have to be my story. I learned that when I realized I couldn't relate to God through my dad's faith or my mother's experience, I had to receive God through His Son, Jesus, for myself and walk out my own life journey.

I am my mother's daughter—but more importantly, I am my Father's daughter. When I asked Jesus to be my Lord and Savior, Father God adopted me as His eternally beloved daughter. I am His image bearer. And He calls me good.

He calls you good too.

"Thus, we have been set free to experience our rightful heritage. You can tell for sure that you are now fully adopted as His own children because God sent the Spirit of His Son into our lives crying out, 'Papa! Father!'" (Galatians 4:5–6 MSG).

In Christ, we are made into reborn creations. Hallelujah! The old has gone and the new has come (2 Corinthians 5:17). Actually, we're better than new. God's Spirit dwells within us. We live and move and have our being in Him (Acts 17:28). And whether we do or do not struggle with mental illness, we have the mind of Christ (1 Corinthians 2:14). Let me repeat that: whether we do or do not struggle with mental illness, God has given us the mind of Christ. Nothing—not our infirmities, our issues, our weaknesses—can separate us from God and His love.

God is *Jehovah Rapha*, the God who heals. He called us to Himself even when we were sinners. Even when we didn't want to know Him. He did that for me. I'm not a super Christian. I'm flawed, still prone to do what I don't want to do, and I don't always do what I should do. I am in process. But I stay in the Word of God. I read it every day, and I ask God to help me live it by His grace and Spirit. I have to. You have to. Sounds simple—but oh the power that is unleashed through the words of the Bible.

Whether we do or do not struggle with mental illness, God has given us the mind of Christ.

"Filling your minds and meditating on things true, noble, reputable, authentic, compelling, gracious—the best, not the worst; the beautiful, not the ugly; things to praise, not things to curse" (Philippians 4:8 MSG).

Worship has been God's special gift to me. I love to proclaim Him in song. I find that when I do, I am made more and more whole. I believe you will discover the same. Singing God's praises sets evil minions fleeing and the angels of God to working. When we sing, we acknowledge the God who took our infirmities upon Himself and promises to fulfill His purpose for us no matter what we go through.

I have had my own bouts of depression—even suicidal thoughts. Not because of my mom or aunt or anybody else. Just life and my own pain and choices. We all have our own stuff. But I know God heals. Whether that is through His miraculous touch, heaven, medicine, treatment, counseling, a loving community, or like with Elijah, through rest and food, God makes a way for us when our identity is in Him and His Word.

Living Truth

Thus, we have been set free to experience our rightful heritage. (Galatians 4:5 MSG)

For He sent His word and healed them. (Psalm 107:20 KJV)

Living Prayer

Father, You made me in Your image. You call me good. I am Yours. Even in my weakness, infirmity, and sin You call me Your beloved daughter. Please comfort me. Manifest Your peace in me. Bring me healing and strength for my days. Remind me that You love me just as I am. I give myself to You. Make me more and more like Jesus. And use me for Your glory. Bless me indeed, Father.

Living Action

You are not your disease. You are not your parents. You are not your status or condition. You are God's beloved daughter, made in His image to do wonderful things that He prepared in advance for you to do. You are good enough.

You are God's beloved daughter, made in His image to do wonderful things that He prepared in advance for you to do.

Do those things that draw you closer to Him. Use your gifts, talents, abilities, and treasure for His glory. Serve God by serving others in His name. Immerse yourself in nature, art, and music. Look for and acknowledge the beauty around you—especially that which lies within you.

- What are some experiences from your family history that have shaped your view of yourself?
- What does God's Word say about who you should pattern yourself after? (See Psalm 119:7 MSG and Philippians 2:1–4 NIV.)
- What can bring peace and transformation—especially in our minds? (See Isaiah 26:3 NIV and Romans 12:2 NIV.)

_____

_____

_____

_____

_____

_____

_____

_____

_____

_____

Denise Ann Goosby has worked as a community reporter and as an educator in public and private schools. In 2018, she founded the nonprofit Healing Song Ministries. She graduated with a masters in nonprofit management from Biola University in May 2020. Her blog, *Denise's Healing Journey,* launched in July 2020. She is single and lives in Southern California.

Chapter Twenty-Four

Preparing for the Storm
Lizann Lightfoot

I knew military life would require me to be flexible and handle a lot during my husband's overseas deployments. But news of a Category 3 hurricane heading toward our town seemed to be too much to handle. Not only was I home alone raising a toddler and a three-year-old, but the hurricane was arriving the same week I was due to deliver baby number three!

All my carefully made birth plans were falling apart as the military base was closing, and the hospital was only open for emergency patients. The friend I had invited to hold my hand in the delivery room was evacuating with her family. In the days before the storm hit, my mind reeled with an internal storm of frustration, anger, and confusion. Delivering a baby on my own during deployment was already intimidating. Why did God have to throw a hurricane into the mix?

On the outside though, I had to remain calm. I went through the motions of storm preparation. I gathered up the outdoor furniture and brought it into the garage. I purchased a tarp and gallons of water. I convinced my parents to make the ten-hour drive *into* the storm zone with a generator so they could stay home with my children. I took daily walks around the neighborhood, trying to convince the baby to come out before the storm. During those walks, I prayed for the strength and courage to face the challenge ahead of me.

If the hurricane had arrived when my first baby was due, I would have panicked. I didn't know anything about birth or recovery, so how could I have juggled that terrible week of being a first-time mom with storm preparations and power outages? Similarly, if there had been hurricane evacuations during my husband's first military deployment, I'm not sure how I would have handled it. At that time, I knew little about military resources or how to find support in the community. But this was not my first deployment, or my first baby. God had given me years to prepare for this challenge. I just never saw it coming.

That's one constant about bad news: it never comes at a convenient time. There is rarely a warning before we learn something devastating that will shake us up and ruin our week. We are always just one phone call away from a family member's illness or death, one ticking sound away from an enormous car repair bill, and one mistake away from losing our phone or being locked out of the house. Trouble happens. There is simply no way to avoid it. And when it comes, we are always left with the question, "What do I do now?"

Some would say the answer to life's challenges is to have faith in God and to pray during times of trouble. Of course, that is good advice, but I don't think it goes deep enough. We all know the verse from Philippians 4:13 (ESV) that says, "I can do all things through him who strengthens me." This is often used as encouragement when someone is facing a difficult situation. But the verse right before it puts it into important context. In verse 12, Paul wrote: "I know how to be brought low, and I know how to abound. In any and every circumstance, I have learned the secret of facing plenty and hunger, abundance and need." Paul reminds us Christ is with us during times of plenty, preparing us to face times of hunger. Christ is the secret to strength.

Just as Joseph in Egypt taught Pharaoh to store up harvests during the bountiful years in preparation for the lean years, God wants us to begin preparing for difficult times *before they happen*. We may not have prophetic dreams to warn us of a coming famine, but we know sooner or later, we are bound to face troubles in life. Just as we use the time before a storm to stock up on canned goods and toilet paper, God wants us to use the

God had given me years to prepare for this challenge. I just never saw it coming.

times of abundance in our lives to draw closer to Him so He can strengthen us for the lean times that will inevitably challenge us.

God wants us to begin preparing for difficult times *before they happen.*

Every military spouse knows there are going to be problems during deployment. You don't know when challenges will come, but you know they will stress you and push you to your limits. All you can do is build up your courage ahead of time so you have the mental fortitude to handle difficulties when they come. We don't wait until someone has fallen into a lake to teach them how to swim. In the same way, even though prayer is a great way to build up your strength and courage, we cannot expect someone going through trauma to pray their way to mental health.

So when my husband prepared for deployments to Afghanistan, I took steps ahead of time to protect my mental health and build up a support system. It's because of my actions before I was even pregnant that I was able to face the ordeal of the hurricane birth.

When preparing for his deployment, I always take specific steps to guard my mental health. I can't afford regular childcare, so I try to reserve at least one day a month where I will get a break from the kids. I spend months reaching out, connecting with friends, and making sure I have their numbers saved in my phone in case of an emergency. By the time the hurricane hit, I already knew other wives in the military unit who checked on me. I was part of a moms' group that made me dinner for a week. And I knew I could rely on my parents for emergency childcare.

Just as Jesus built His ministry with the apostles, every Christian should carefully surround themselves with a select handful of close friends and prayer warriors. Build up these supports during healthy times so you can lean on them during challenging days.

Similarly, just as Christ took time to go apart by Himself and rest, we all need to know principles of self-care. What routines refresh or energize you when you are feeling drained?

Previous deployments taught me what works best for me: journaling, writing letters, taking walks, and drinking tea are daily rituals that keep me grounded. Bible study, moms' groups, going to church, and phone dates with my best friend are

> Just as Jesus built His ministry with the apostles, every Christian should carefully surround themselves with a select handful of close friends and prayer warriors.

weekly routines that refresh me when my husband is away. If I get tired and skip these activities, my mental health suffers. It is easy to slip into depression or anxiety when I am home alone raising young children. I have learned that these simple self-care rituals are an essential part of my mental health routine. I have to take them seriously because I never know what mental health challenge I am training for next.

Because of my years of unknowing preparation, I had the strength I needed to give birth alone during a hurricane. My plans had to pivot, but I made one decision and step at a time.

My son was born at night, while Hurricane Isabelle whipped the trees outside the hospital windows. Once he was born, I had a rush of joy and relief! I didn't know God had made me that strong, but it opened my eyes to the incredible untapped potential for strength within each woman. Military wives often say, "You never know how strong you are until being strong is your only choice." God is always our strength, during times of abundance and times of need.

◡ *Living Truth*

When you pass through the waters, I will be with you; and through the rivers, they shall not overwhelm you; when you walk through fire you shall not be burned, and the flame shall not consume you. (Isaiah 43:2 ESV)

◡ *Living Prayer*

Lord, I thank You for being my constant support in times of need. On the good days, I ask You to remind me of Your presence so I know You are always with me. On my bad days, I ask You to be with me and share Your strength and courage so I can face the mighty challenges in my path.

I didn't know God had made me that strong, but it opened my eyes to the incredible untapped potential for strength within each woman.

∼ *Living Action*

- Who are your prayer warriors or inner circle that you would turn to if you received bad news?
- What is one routine or habit you can add to your week that makes you feel stronger and more prepared to handle anything?

_____

_____

_____

_____

_____

_____

_____

_____

_____

_____

_____

_____

_____

Lizann Lightfoot is a Christian military spouse, mom of five kids, a published author, and a speaker. She loves sharing hope and encouragement with the military community, especially during deployments. Visit her blog at SeasonedSpouse.com, or find her on social media as the Seasoned Spouse.

Part 5

Suffering

Chapter Twenty-Five

When Hard Presses Us into Healing
Debbie Alsdorf

Ann Voskamp wrote, "Maybe wholeness is embracing brokenness as part of your life."[5]

I stood frozen at the kitchen counter, wishing I could find something to ease my pain. The cupboard above me held nothing to help the defeat coursing through every part of me. It wasn't a headache—it was a heartache.

I can pinpoint the day my heart broke into a million little pieces. The shattering of my life left wounds in my soul—embarrassing, gaping wounds that left me questioning every single thing about myself. I was blindsided. My husband of nearly fourteen years said he never loved me. Never? Yes, that was his truth, never.

Was every memory wasted? The anniversary trips. The nights of passion. The tender cards he wrote me. Was every act of love a sham? What about our two children? Were they conceived in love? I thought so.

Everything I believed and hoped in was gone. Our family was forever changed, as was my identity as a woman, wife, and pastor's wife. Who was I now that I could no longer rely on who I had been? The pain was real, and the suffering that was going on inside my heart could not be soothed nor fully understood by another person. I was beginning to learn the pain we feel alone is the hardest suffering of all. The death of our dreams and the breaking of our hearts is a hard thing to endure.

Like anyone who is suffering, I had questions. *Why God? Couldn't You have stopped this?* Rejection ripped through me, and I was drowning in nauseating fear, doubt, and pain. I had been a ministry leader, but here I was slipping into the pit of depression, a pit I had never dreamed of being in.

It wasn't the first time I'd been rejected, and it wouldn't be the last. Each heartbreak brings with it a familiar pain.

There is no quick and easy answer for suffering. There is no fast-acting pill to undo the wounds dangling ragged in a heart.

Fast-forward years later to my cancer diagnosis. Once again I had questions. *It's common*, I thought. *It's caught early*, I reasoned. But when the treatments began and my breast was cut up to save the rest of me, my nice reasonings went out the window. When you are suffering something out of your control, it is easy to feel that maybe God has rejected you and turned away from you.

"Why, God?" I asked, "Why? Couldn't You have spared me this cancer cup?"

God's answer to my heart was tender: *Yes, I can do all things. But, dear one, when I don't remove the cup, I have something for you in that cup.*

What? Something for me in the cup of cancer? Ridiculous, I thought. Over time, it became clear that if something passes through my life, not only is God with me but He is for me. He is powerful enough to work good out of the bad and beauty out of the ugly. Daring to believe this began to change me.

The truth is we will all experience hard things before our story is over. Jesus speaking to His disciples said, "In this world you will have trouble. But take heart! I have overcome the world" (John 16:33 NIV).

This word *trouble* in the original Greek is a word that means "a pressing together or pressure, tribulation, affliction, anguish, persecution, and burdens." Suffering, according to *Webster's Dictionary*, is: "the state or experience of one who suffers, pain, hardship."

And though none of us wants to suffer, it is best to come to the place of

> **I was beginning to learn the pain we feel alone is the hardest suffering of all.**

understanding that sometimes life is filled with trouble. This is real life, as relevant today as it was thousands of years ago.

Yes, I can do all things. But, dear one, when I don't remove the cup, I have something for you in that cup.

We have all known hard. It wrings out faith like a wet rag, leaving questions that we have no answers for. Regardless of what has happened or how things played out, suffering is all-consuming and affects all of us.

Hard will press us into God or lead us into despair—sometimes a little of both. What if we could learn to embrace the beauty in our brokenness? What if we could find Christ in our personal cups of suffering? What if God's love for us could become so real that it is the foundation we stand on in the middle of all trouble?

I needed to learn that Jesus was my tender healer and that He would redeem every broken place in me. Maybe you can relate.

Suffering introduces us to a place called "the meantime." The meantime is that place in between a problem recognized and its solution realized. It is the dash between point A and point B. The meantime is part of life, whether it is getting through the day or getting through the next few months or years. And, if we are going to be real, the meantimes in life are often *mean*.

As I sought God for grace, answers, and renewed faith, I began to realize life can unravel people or bring them to a continual place of greater peace. I was in the unraveled club and desperately needed to learn how to walk in peace and victory in the midst of sufferings, big and small.

I wish I could tell you that a divorce was the only thing that unraveled me. Or I could sweeten the story with how I learned great lessons, practiced spiritual disciplines like forgiveness, and went on my merry way. That is not my story.

I never dreamed of being the poster child for emotional pain, depression, divorce, loss, or illness. And I never dreamed of being in the pink club as a breast cancer survivor. Yet each of these are part of my story. Each pain is a chapter unto itself, but each one was ultimately used by God to eventually strengthen me, rather than destroy me.

Life has been littered with hard and showered with good. The gap between the two is often confusing and painful. Here are some of the things I have learned along the way:

- When bad things happen, God is still in control.
- Other people make choices that affect me, but God is still with me.
- I cannot control circumstances, but I can trust God with the details.
- Problems are inevitable, but living overwhelmed is optional.
- I am not alone, but held and loved by God.
- God holds me together, even when things are falling apart.
- There is a plan, even when it looks like there isn't.
- Things happened to me, so something can happen in me.

Because we are human, questions still loom. "Why God? Did You hear my prayer? Do You see my need? Did You see what *they* did to me? Don't You care? Can't You stop all of this?"

And, yes, He can do all things. But when He doesn't, there is something for us in the hard. I began to see every hard cup as a giving cup. In every cup of life, God desires to give us the gift of Himself. In hard times my question began to change from "Why, God?" to "What, God? What will Your gift be in this current circumstance?" This became a radically new perspective for me and began changing how I view the hard things that come into my life.

In *Streams in the Desert* I read, "If you have surrendered yourself to Christ, your present circumstances that seem to be pressing so hard against you are the perfect tool in the Father's hand to chisel you into shape for eternity."[6]

∿ Living Truth

I consider that our present sufferings are not worth comparing with the glory that will be revealed in us. (Romans 8:18 NIV)

And we know that in all things God works for the good of those who love him, who have been called according to his purpose. For those God foreknew he also predestined to be conformed to the likeness of his Son. (Romans 8:28–29 NIV)

What then shall we say in response to these things? If God is for us, who can be against us? (Romans 8:31 NIV)

No, in all things we are more than conquerors through him who loved us. For I am convinced that neither death nor life, neither angels or demons, neither the present nor the future, nor any powers, neither height nor depth, nor anything else in all creation, will be able to separate us from the love of God that is in Christ Jesus our Lord. (Romans 8:37–39 NIV)

In every cup of life,
God desires to give us
the gift of Himself.

~ Living Prayer

Dear Jesus, I come to You with all the hard, brittle broken parts of me. I know You are with me and will never leave me. I accept that troubles are part of life and suffering will be part of the story here on earth. Thank You for the promise of shaping me through hard things, and the promise that nothing will be wasted in the life of those who love You. I thank You that nothing can separate me from Your love. No depression, rejection, loss, circumstance, or disease will turn You away from me. Today remind me frequently of Your great and enduring love for me. Today remind me that I am enough because You live within me and You are enough, no matter what I walk through. Today remind me that You make beauty out of brokenness and joy in the midst of sorrow. Today remind me that You will hold my hand in every grief and walk me through every valley. I praise You that You are my Shepherd and that goodness and mercy will follow me all the days of my life. My cup is full, even in suffering. I have no need to fear. Remind me often of this overflowing cup and Your enduring love.

~ Living Action

In what way are you currently walking through trouble or suffering? Have you believed that your problems were too big for God? Have you felt your cup was empty even though Scripture says it is overflowing?

When we are going through hard times, spiritual practices become very important. Here are some of the things that I have had to incorporate during the hard seasons in my story. Journal about each one and how it can help you get through your current circumstances.

- Have faith that your problems can be a positive growth experience.
- Learn to believe in the giving cup that Christ holds out for us.
- Ask for courage to live one day at a time.
- Stay in God's Word, even if it is just one portion of Scripture or one psalm.
- Refuse anxiety and pray instead.
- Look for good, find the good, and dwell there.
- Remember God's love for you, morning, noon, and night, and every hour in between.

_____

_____

_____

_____

_____

_____

Debbie Alsdorf's mission is to lead women to the heart of God's love, through the truth of His Word. She is an international speaker, the author of twelve books, and featured on the Aspire Women's Events Tour. After a lifetime in California, Debbie and her husband Ray now make their home in Arizona. They have raised a blended family of four children and have nine grandlittles who call her Grammy. Visit her at debbiealsdorf.com.

Chapter Twenty-Six

Trusting God When We Don't Understand
Missy Linkletter

On July 15, 2017, our lives changed forever. It was 5:00 a.m. when the incessant ringing of the doorbell jarred us awake. My husband and I both assumed our twenty-year-old son must have locked himself out of the house. As my husband went downstairs to open the door, I stood on the landing, waiting to hear Justin apologizing for waking us up at such an hour. Instead, I heard unfamiliar muffled voices and my husband inviting someone into our home.

I rushed down the stairs in my pajamas and immediately faced two grim-faced sheriff's deputies.

"What is it? What's the matter? Where's Justin?" I asked.

"Ma'am, we are sorry to inform you that your son was killed in a car accident last night."

The room swirled around me as I tried with all of my might to wake up from what must be a terrible nightmare. Just as I was on the edge of hysteria, our three youngest sons stood before me pajama-clad and blurry-eyed.

"Mama," they cried, "what's wrong? What's going on, Mama?"

I pulled them in close and prayed for the words to say to their precious little hearts. How could I tell them that their big brother, their hero, was gone?

As soon as the sheriff's deputies left, we began making phone calls. The first on our list was our daughter, who was working at a summer camp three hours away. Justin and Sarah were best friends, and at only two and a half years apart, they did everything together. Because of social media, we needed to reach her before the word spread. It was one of the most anguishing moments of my life.

In our earliest days of grief, friends and family surrounded us. Their presence was a healing balm to our souls. But when the meal train ended, and the final sympathy card was received, I could not accept our new normal. How could I move forward without my firstborn? I prayed, but I had no peace. I tried to read my Bible, but the words seemed to bounce off the pages. I physically ached for my son, and a gulf of anguish filled my soul. I was nearing despair, and with my mind so loud, I could not sense the Lord's nearness.

The Bible tells us that I was not alone in my anguish. Among biblical characters, no one besides Jesus endured more suffering than a man named Job, a blameless and upright man who feared God and turned away from evil. Job was the father of ten children, seven sons and three daughters. He was a wealthy man with a significant number of servants and livestock. Job was a diligent father who made morning sacrifices on his children's behalf just in case "they cursed God in their hearts" (Job 1:5 esv).

One day, Satan presented himself before the Lord.

> The Lord said to Satan, "From where have you come?" Satan answered the Lord and said, "From going to and fro on the earth, and from walking up and down on it." And the Lord said to Satan, "Have you considered my servant Job, that there is none like him on the earth, a blameless and upright man, who fears God and turns away from evil?" (Job 1:7–8 esv)

```
I was nearing despair,
and with my mind so
loud, I could not sense
the Lord's nearness.
```

Satan went on to accuse Job, saying the only reason he was faithful was because of God's abundant blessings upon him. Satan was sure that once the Lord took away all that he had, Job would curse him to his face.

`I knew the Lord as my refuge, my comforter, and my protector. But when we lost Justin, I was bewildered.`

The Lord told Satan, "Behold, all that he has is in your hand. Only against him do not stretch out your hand" (Job 1:12 ESV).

In one day, without warning, Job's ten children died, he lost all of his livestock, and the majority of his servants perished. When Job received the news, he shaved his head, tore his robe, fell on the ground, and worshiped, saying, "Naked I came from my mother's womb, and naked shall I return. The Lord gave, and the Lord has taken away; blessed be the name of the Lord" (Job 1:20 ESV). The Bible tells us that in all this Job did not sin.

Again Satan went before the Lord and accused Job. Once more, God permitted Satan to sift Job. For a second time, our beloved Job experienced affliction. This time he had painful sores from the soles of his feet to the crown of his head. Job's wife was of little comfort and said, "Do you still hold fast to your integrity? Curse God and die" (Job 2:9 ESV).

For months, Job languished in his misery. His wife was repulsed by his disfigurement, and even little children despised him. Just when things seemed like they couldn't get any worse, Job's three friends entered. When they heard of all the evil that befell Job, they went to him to offer sympathy and comfort. Because they couldn't understand why such calamity visited Job, they accused him of grievously sinning against the Lord.

Job responded, "Though He slay me, I will hope in him; yet I will argue my ways to his face" (Job 13:15 ESV). And still, Job himself could not comprehend why devastation came upon his household. Job drew his conclusions for his suffering; he accused God of being unjust. Have you ever felt like Job?

When I was fifteen years old, I placed my faith in Jesus Christ. My new life in Him was a stark contrast to the darkness of my old reality. As my faith deepened,

> It's as if He took my cheeks in His hands and said, "Missy, you're never going to understand this, but trust in me with all of your heart."

I knew the Lord as my refuge, my comforter, and my protector. But when we lost Justin, I was bewildered.

You see, I prayed for Justin's safety the day of the accident. I prayed for him well into the night, asking God to protect him.

I couldn't understand what went wrong. Finally, late one night, all of my anguish reached a fever-pitch, and I accused God, saying, "Lord, why would Justin only be allotted twenty years on this earth? He wanted to be a pastor; he loved You. Lord, I asked You to keep him safe. Why didn't You keep him safe?"

I, like Job, didn't understand God's plan.

The Lord had an answer for Job. He appeared to Job in a whirlwind and said: "Who is this that darkens counsel by words without knowledge? Dress for action like a man; I will question you, and you make it known to me" (Job 38:1–3 ESV).

God examined Job. He asked Job if he could explain how the world was created. Did Job govern its creation and its creatures? Could Job compare to His splendid majesty? And who was Job next to the infinite wisdom of Almighty God?

Job wisely replied, "I have uttered what I did not understand, things too wonderful for me, which I did not know" (Job 42:3 ESV).

Just as the Lord answered Job in his despair, so the Lord answered me in my desperation. In the quiet of the night, He took my shattered heart and ministered to me with His Word. He brought to mind Proverbs 3:5, "Trust in the Lord with all of your heart, and do not lean on your own understanding." It's as if He took my cheeks in His hands and said, "Missy, you're never going to understand this, but trust in me with all of your heart." Even though it wasn't the answer I wanted, it was the answer I needed.

Maybe your world has been turned on its side, and nothing makes much sense to you right now. Perhaps you are tempted to despair because you cannot understand why God has allowed you to suffer. Stand firm in your faith, dear Christian. We don't trust God because we understand His plans; we trust in Him because He is God. No matter what our emotions shout, God is always faithful.

~ Living Truth

For he wounds, but he binds up; he shatters, but his hands heal. (Job 5:18 ESV)

I love you, O Lord, my strength. (Psalm 18:1 ESV)

~ Living Prayer

Dearest Lord, the night is dark, and the pain is nearly unbearable. I run to You with my shattered heart. There is no sweeter refuge than You. Please comfort me with Your presence and hide me under the shelter of Your wings. Father, I don't pretend to understand Your plan. Please help me to trust You with my whole heart. I love You, Oh Lord, my strength.

We don't trust God
because we understand
His plans; we trust in
Him because He is God.

～ *Living Action*

- What conclusions have you come to about God amid your season of suffering?
- Do your thoughts line up with the truth of the Scripture? Oftentimes our emotions lag miles behind the truth of Scripture. Take heart. "The Lord is merciful and gracious, slow to anger and abounding in steadfast love" (Psalm 103:8).
- Pour out your heart to Him and yield to His tender care.

_____

_____

_____

_____

_____

_____

_____

_____

_____

_____

_____

_____

Missy Linkletter is the wife of Tim and the mother of five children: four boys and one girl. She's an aspiring author, a conference speaker, a Bible teacher, and a student of the Word. You can connect with her at missy linkletter.com, Facebook, and Instagram.

Chapter Twenty-Seven

The Road to Healing from Oppression
Cheryl Lutz

I earnestly interceded and claimed the shed blood of Jesus over my mind and body as the worship service was under way. *I am a child of God; you have no power over me*, I silently but boldly declared. My body began to tremble as I called upon God the Father to "glorify His name" in my affliction.

Right on the heels of that silent prayer, my dear pastor and husband read: "'Father, glorify Your name!' Then a voice came from heaven, 'I have glorified it, and will glorify it again'" (John 12:28 NIV).

Contemplating that moment still gives me chills. After my husband read John 12:28, the oppression intensified, and I could feel my body beginning to crumble. I stumbled to the sanctuary door to make my escape. I fell in the hallway, and my Nalgene bottle bounced onto the tile floor, causing a cacophony of noise. Faithful friends leaped from their seats to help me into the church library. My eyes rolled back in my head, deep guttural sounds escaped from my throat, and my limbs jerked uncontrollably. The average onlooker would assume I was having a grand mal seizure.

Yet, several years before this, when I experienced these provoked convulsions while hooked up to an EEG monitor in the hospital, the electrical activity in my brain appeared normal, with no spikes or sharp waves. There were no abnormal, rhythmic discharges of neurons to indicate an epileptic seizure.

Twenty years earlier when my bizarre symptoms began, the neurologists referred to them as pseudo-seizures. However, that term is no longer "politically correct." Non-epileptic seizures or a non-epileptic event is currently considered more correct. Some doctors believe the symptoms may be an attempt to reduce anxiety by not recognizing or responding to an emotional conflict.

But where do mental health, physical symptoms, and spiritual oppression intersect? There is not a simple answer. We must never imply that a person with epilepsy has a demon, or that a seizure is always a sign of a mental health disorder.

Yet for myself, the first several years of my affliction were spent obsessing over the physical. I desperately sought an organic diagnosis, feeling driven to prove to the medical community that I wasn't crazy. I was a Christian, a pastor's wife, a Bible study teacher. How could I possibly have mental health issues that would manifest in such an extreme way? Also, I couldn't accept that spiritual oppression affected a born-again believer in such a fashion.

Yet when I began to acknowledge that my past was affecting my present, the road to healing began.

I was raised in a dysfunctional home by two parents who loved me but were products of their own dysfunctional upbringing. My dad was an alcoholic who self-medicated his mental health issues, and, for as long as I can remember, my mother struggled with depression. Neither of them grew up with healthy role models. As a result, they had a terrible marriage without a foundation of trust or kindness. I grew up with incredible insecurity, crippling anxiety, and over-whelming shyness that followed me into my early adult years.

My eyes rolled back in my head, deep guttural sounds escaped from my throat, and my limbs jerked uncontrollably. The average onlooker would assume I was having a grand mal seizure.

The loneliness, fear, and isolation I experienced as a child left me vulnerable to the lies of the enemy of my soul. I believed in his slanderous words that I was unworthy, stupid, and would never receive unconditional love.

These deep-seated lies led to my experimenting with drugs as well as abusing alcohol in my teen years. I was likewise so consumed with people-pleasing that I participated in a middle school party's seance due to my fear of being rejected if I refused.

The loneliness, fear, and isolation I experienced as a child left me vulnerable to the lies of the enemy of my soul.

My reckless decisions did not give the Evil One possession of my soul because I had already submitted my life to Christ when I was in the sixth grade. However, my sin and unbelief and the opening of demonic portals did lead to extreme oppression. As I unknowingly took the Enemy's lies to heart, the truths of what Christ said about me in His Word were more head knowledge than real heart knowledge.

That morning in the church library began a series of several prayer meetings interceding for my deliverance. The final session was with a therapist and a dear friend. They battled with me in prayer, rebuking the lies the Enemy spewed forth through my mouth and replacing them with the truth of what the Father said about me, as one who is saved by the blood of the Lamb.

Again, where do the physical, mental/emotional, and spiritual collide or divide? We are created with a body, mind, and spirit. A beautiful Creator so intertwined all three areas, it is hard to know where one ends and another begins.

Regarding the physical, I have an autoimmune disease with measurable symptoms, for which I undergo monthly treatments. And separately, my current neurologist believes I have epileptic as well as non-epileptic seizures and has me on an anticonvulsant.

Regarding the emotional and mental health side, I wrestle with anxiety, now brought under control through psychotherapy and medication. I've also done eye movement desensitization and reprocessing (EMDR) therapy. I have painstakingly cleaned out old wounds and reprocessed traumatic memories.

Lastly, regarding the spiritual realm, I've discovered there is a lie from the Enemy we have unknowingly believed at the root of all unresolved wounds and traumatic memories. The same is valid for sin struggles that we can't seem to break free from. Going back and addressing the lies and replacing them with the truths of Scripture closes the door to any access the Enemy has gained in our lives. The

Going back and addressing the lies and replacing them with the truths of Scripture closes the door to any access the Enemy has gained in our lives.

freedom, peace, victory, and soul restoration this painful process brings is glorious.

After years of suffering, I realized my issues are threefold: physical, emotional, spiritual. I have had to address each facet.

The same can be true of you, dear reader. Yet, help, hope, and healing are your portion as well.

In Deuteronomy 33:12 (NIV), Moses addressed the twelve tribes of Israel. About Benjamin, he said, "Let the beloved of the Lord rest secure in him, for he shields him all day long, and the one the Lord loves, rests between His shoulders."

I have now experienced in my heart the truth that I am "beloved of the Lord." I know who I am. My identity is secure. He is my shield, the lifter of my head, despite any physical ailments or daily battles I face.

In Him I am safe and protected from the attacks of the enemy of my soul. I can climb up on my heavenly Daddy's back and find physical, emotional, and spiritual rest, between His shoulders.

 Living Truth

And the God of all grace, who called you to his eternal glory in Christ, after you have suffered a little while, will himself restore you and make you strong, firm and steadfast. (1 Peter 5:10 NIV)

～ *Living Prayer*

Father, You came to seek and to save that which was lost and set captives free. Lord, though weapons are formed against us by the Evil One and we suffer, we trust the Enemy's evil intentions will not prosper. May we rest in the fact that Christ securely holds us in suffering, and that Your grace is enough. Thank You that You waste no pain and our tears are not in vain as You collect them in a bottle. And we rejoice that one day our weeping will end as we join Your Son, our blood-bought advocate, in our heavenly home. Come quickly, Lord Jesus!

～ *Living Action*

- In what ways are you suffering because of lies you have believed?
- Are you holding on to areas of unforgiveness?
- Do you have trusted friends or a counselor who can come alongside and pray God's truth over you, teaching you to rebuke the lies of the Enemy and embrace what God says about you?

My sin and unbelief and the opening of demonic portals did lead to extreme oppression.

Remember, there is no shame in seeking out a trusted Christian therapist. You can be free from the lies from your past. Let God's light shine on your hidden secrets. Exposing them to the light of Christ breaks their power. Then step into His love, knowing you're securely held in Him.

_____

_____

_____

_____

_____

_____

_____

_____

_____

_____

_____

_____

_____

_____

Cheryl Lutz is the founder of Securely Held. She helps Christian women with hidden secrets find the deliverance that only God offers. Her passion is helping others realize Christ firmly holds them amid spiritual warfare. She is a pastor's wife with four adult children and a bonus son by marriage. You can find her at CherylLutz.com, Facebook, and Instagram.

Chapter Twenty-Eight

Forgiving Myself
Jacqueline Middler

My story begins with a desperate act of fear that produced a lifetime of suffering. It wasn't until I was able to truly understand God and His mercy that I could release myself from my prison of suffering.

I looked down at the skinny white stick dripping with my urine and watched as the liquid spread to the two tiny ovals. Immediately, a line formed in the first box. I clenched my eyes and prayed that the other line would not appear. Less than a second later, the other line appeared and confirmed my worst fears.

I was pregnant.

My eyes started to swim with unshed tears. I threw the stick on the counter and grabbed the box, attempting to read the directions through the blur. After repeatedly looking from the directions to the stick and back again, the truth hit me. I gasped. *This can't be happening to me!*

I was a nineteen-year-old freshman in college, looking at a little white stick that would change my life in three short minutes.

The next ten days brought me angst as I tried to decide what to do. In my inner heart I knew abortion was wrong, but I was desperate. The fear I felt was overwhelming. The unknown of what having this baby would do to my life was paralyzing.

I was a nineteen-year-old freshman in college, looking at a little white stick that would change my life in three short minutes.

Finally, I made the choice, the choice the law said was legal, but my soul said was not.

I quieted all the doubt and fear and lied to myself and killed my baby.

From the moment I watched the doctor put the instruments inside of me and suck out that little life, I was changed. My whole soul and life shattered in that one instant. I thought by making this choice I was freeing myself; little did I know the suffering I would endure.

There are many different types of suffering. One type is the hell of self-afflicted torment. The beauty of life is that we all have choice—it's called free will. The nightmare begins when we use our free will to harm ourselves and others. People who cause their own suffering live in a cycle of shame and guilt that can bind them for years.

Unable to reconcile the pieces of myself as a person who killed her baby, I used drugs and alcohol at a rate that was sure to kill me. Within a year I was pregnant again, and my life was spinning out of control. I was on a fast track to death and didn't know where the brakes were.

This time the choice to abort was harder to make, but I went ahead anyway. Fear was my motivator, the unknown my god. The chains I strung around my life were tight, and I was drowning in a pit of despair.

After the second abortion, my soul hid deep behind a hardened wall as I lost all hope.

The suffering I brought onto myself exchanged my wide, innocent, and mischievous eyes for hardened, untrusting, bitter ones. My once-long honey-kissed blonde hair was now chopped off and a hard red. My teeth were no longer white but stained yellow from all the cigarettes I smoked. The plump cheeks of my youth were exchanged for harsher features due to the corrosion in my soul. There was nothing innocent, nothing pure in my face, only emptiness. I was lost in a sea of shame and guilt.

This is the person God came to save, not the wide-eyed innocent girl who had gotten a full scholarship to school. I was now the girl who had slept with countless people, who had killed two innocents, who had done things she said she never would. I was a broken, hopeless, suffering soul.

When my desperate eyes sought some form of help, my God showed up. He came and spoke His loving words to me. As I started to read the Bible, His words came alive. The fear that had trapped me unraveled. As I said yes to God, I felt for the first time in my life a beacon of hope for my soul.

I wish I could say my shame and guilt went instantly away, and that I forgave myself in that moment, but that was not the case. I suffered in silent shame and guilt for many years to come.

I spent the first years of my Christian walk trying to understand God and His love. I pored over His Word and spent time in prayer. I let the demons of shame and guilt live locked away in the broken part of my heart. I could accept God's forgiveness but could not accept my own.

God allowed me to stay locked in my own unforgiveness while He gently tugged on the hidden parts of my heart. He was patient and blessed me with daughters and a son of my own.

When I saw their ultrasounds, I felt joy and despair, guilt and awe. Each pregnancy allowed a little bit of my grief to come out. God's Word and the baby in my arms helped me not to dwell in my despair.

During that time I had two miscarriages and struggled with thinking that was retribution for my choices. God's Spirit directed me to His Word, and in it I read words of love and grace.

About fourteen years after becoming a Christian, I was reading through the Bible and came to the Ten Commandments. As I read through the list I had read many times before, the words "You shall not murder" struck me. My eyes blurred, and I froze. I had never connected the dots before.

I am a murderer.

I knew I had chosen to kill those babies but had never recognized that it made me a murderer. The wall holding my sorrow and silent suffering in and

I thought by making this choice I was freeing myself; little did I know the suffering I would endure.

away from the outside world crashed down, and I began to cry. I cried for my babies, for myself, and for all the bad choices I had made.

When the last tear fell, I looked up and asked God, "How can you love me knowing these horrible things about me?"

He did not answer me with harsh judgment, nor did I feel a stony silence. Instead, I felt His Spirit fill me with peace.

Of all the steps I had taken so far on my journey, this was the first step to forgiving myself and to no longer suffering in silence. I took full responsibility for what I had done. No more hiding. I had to face the shame and the guilt and no longer punish myself. I looked at myself in the mirror and admitted, "I can forgive you."

The God of the universe forgave me after I had chosen to murder two of His souls, and for all the other bad decisions I made, one after another, because of my choice to murder—abusing alcohol and drugs, alienating friends, choosing bad partners, screwing up good jobs, the list goes on and on. Once I realized His full forgiveness for me, I was able to allow the bindings I put on my soul to fall away.

I opened the Bible and found David, who was used by God to lead His people. David had murdered his best friend after he slept with his wife and got her pregnant. When I read God called David a man after His own heart, I felt hope—hope that God could use me and had a plan for my life.

I knew I was forgiven, but I had never felt trusted. Then I looked to Jesus and saw in His ministry He used the desperate, the broken, and the hurting. I no longer had to suffer for the death of my two babies. Jesus's blood had paid the price, and I was finally free.

With freedom comes courage and hope. While I punished myself for the lives I took, I was unable to live the life God had called me to. When we hold on to our pain, we allow the Evil One to trap us in shame and guilt.

> God allowed me to stay locked in my own unforgiveness while He gently tugged on the hidden parts of my heart.

Some of the women who have made this choice know the hurt runs deep, although it may be hidden. It is a bleeding, sorrowful wound that seeps shame, guilt, and bitterness into every part of our lives.

Once we come out of hiding and acknowledge our choice to abort, we are no longer trapped. Then we can fill this wound with God's words of love to us.

```
Once I realized His full
forgiveness for me, I
was able to allow the
bindings I put on my
soul to fall away.
```

 *Living Truth*

But when the kindness and love of God our Savior appeared, he saved us, not because of righteous things we had done, but because of his mercy. He saved us through the washing of rebirth and renewal by the Holy Spirit, whom he poured out on us generously through Jesus Christ our Savior, so that, having been justified by his grace, we might become heirs having the hope of eternal life. (Titus 3:4–7 NIV)

Living Prayer

Holy Father, You alone are the Creator of all things and You deserve all power and glory. You are faithful in Your ability to carry out what You say. You are worthy of all praise. We come before You broken and suffering, having taken a precious life and being locked in our shame and guilt. Help us to release our feelings, for there is no condemnation for those in Jesus. You do not want us to carry around guilt for our actions but to have freedom from sin. Your precious Son's blood covers over every vile thing we do and makes us pure and holy. We no longer fear death or punishment and are now blameless in Your sight. Help us trust You enough to forgive ourselves.

Living Action

If, like me, you have had an abortion, you may wonder if you could ever really be forgiven. You may feel like you must treat yourself a certain way because of your decision. You may believe you are not allowed to grieve for your babies, that you shouldn't talk about your choice. You may feel like you will be met with judgment and condemnation. However, hiding those feelings and suffering in silence only leads to death. Jesus's sacrifice on the cross is meant to free us from our sin and suffering. He has removed your sin and sees you in a different light. You are forgiven.

When we hold on to our
pain, we allow the Evil
One to trap us in shame
and guilt.

- Describe how it makes you feel to know that God sees you without your sin.
- Do you understand the extent of God's love for you? Describe what that means to you.
- Are you able to forgive yourself, knowing you are forgiven?
- Do you believe you no longer have to suffer for your actions?

_____

_____

_____

_____

_____

_____

_____

_____

_____

_____

An avid reader and devoted mother of three, Jacqueline Middler gives voice to the women who have had abortions and live with the regret and shame of that decision. She has a degree from Johnson & Wales in marketing, with concentrations in English and psychology. Jacqueline works in the meetings industry as an independent contractor helping her clients find and contract hotels and resorts for their meetings and events. She is a trained stillbirth doula working with families of fatal fetal diagnosis and pregnancy loss at any stage. She volunteers with her local pregnancy choice center helping women by sharing the love of Jesus and her story.

Chapter Twenty-Nine

Tender Words in the Wilderness
Jenn Dafoe-Turner

As I stood in the security line at the airport, tears streamed down my face as questions screamed for my attention. *When will I be home? Will I be okay? Can I actually do this?*

I was walking into the unknown after saying goodbye to my husband Ken and our children. Afraid, I silently prayed, *I need this to work. Lord, I need You to work—You are my only hope.*

In my mind I replayed what the blond social worker said as she sat across the table from me. I could see her mouth moving, but the words I was hearing were not lining up with her facial expressions. "One week. You have one week, or we will take your children."

It was as if the words "One week . . . take your children" echoed in my mind.

This was my bottom. I felt face down in the dirt, hedged in, stripped naked, vulnerable, afraid. I could not fall any further than where I was.

I often wonder if Gomer in the Bible felt like this. Gomer was the prostitute who the prophet Hosea married under the direction of the Lord. The writer tells us that Gomer was hedged in with a thicket of thorns, and she was stripped naked. The Lord said He would block her path with a wall to make her lose her way. In great detail, the Word tells how Gomer would suffer for her choices. When I read her story, something in my spirit keeps saying, "Oh, wow. That's me."

There I stood at the airport, broken, "naked," vulnerable, and filled with shame. I was off to Prince Edward Island with a one-way ticket in hand. No return date. My only mission was to get sober. I had been drowning my anger, guilt, and shame with drugs and alcohol, and I was exhausted and could not run anymore.

Standing in that airport lineup in my hazy reality, God gave me a vision of Jesus cradling me in His arms, whispering into my ear, as my head nestled into the crook of His neck, *Your time in the wilderness is finished.*

I knew I was going to be okay. My suffering was coming to an end; I was coming home. I was weeping because of the great swell of hope I was experiencing, for the first time in a long time, from this vision of restoration and redemption.

Jesus was giving me another chance.

I had fallen head over heels in love with Jesus back in 1997. I had never heard the message of Jesus presented in such a way that pricked my heart as it did the day the Lord called my name. He said, "It is time, Jennifer."

I had to turn my head to see who was talking to me. I was sitting in the far back pew, the one closest to the door. I call it the most unholy spot in the church, because I knew what I was, and I knew I didn't belong in that church. I also sat in this spot because I could get out the door fast when the service ended.

That sweet Sunday morning of December 6, 1997, I said the "big yes." I gave Jesus my heart and life that day and said goodbye to a life of sin. I began to soak up God and His Word like a sponge. Growing in leaps and bounds, I felt the nudge to become a pastor at one of our district assemblies. I said yes, even though I was filled with doubt and insecurities. I mean, after all, I was the nobody that nobody wanted, I was the failure who never finished anything. But, out of obedience, I went to school and finished. I prepared. I did my part. And then God invited me into the privilege of suffering with Him for a period, and I missed it.

I was walking into the unknown after saying goodbye to my husband Ken and our children.

Our church came under massive spiritual attack causing so much turmoil and strife that I no longer wanted to be there. It seemed to be one hurt after another. I could not understand why. Why was God not answering my prayer and addressing the issues? Surely the things I was witnessing did not line up with Scripture. People's attitudes, mine included, were not in line with the Word of God, and I perceived Him to be doing nothing about it.

> I had been drowning my anger, guilt, and shame with drugs and alcohol, and I was exhausted and could not run anymore.

At the same time, in my personal life, our family went through a tremendous amount of loss, the death of my father-in-law being one. I was done. I was angry at the Lord. I thought, *If this is what serving You is like, I am good. I will pass.*

I left the church. It was mutually agreed that my district minister's license would not be renewed. I was finished.

I didn't understand the concept of suffering with God. Or the fact that it is a privilege when we get to suffer with God.

I was so angry at God that, out of spite, I took back everything He had healed me from: smoking, drinking, and drugs. However, it was the day I got arrested for assault that I had finally put enough sin in between my Lord and me that I could no longer hear Him.

I continued to walk in this dark path for the next five years as addiction overtook me. I took many dangerous risks, exploring lifestyles that I never dreamed of, same-sex relationships, and prostitution.

I thank God often for protecting me from myself. I have grown to love how God weaves His tapestry in our lives while we are unaware but see it in hindsight.

As I sat on the edge of my bed with my pile of weed on one side of my night table and a beer on the other side, I remember thinking *I don't want to live*, but I did not want to die either. As I watched the smoke twirl up in the air, I was genuinely dead inside and wished to disappear like the smoke. I felt completely and utterly hopeless and full of despair.

That night as my husband put me to bed, as he had so many nights, he did something different, he laid over me and prayed, "Lord, if You fix her, I am Yours forever." When I first listened to my husband tell this, I could hear the suffering in his voice. When I misunderstood the invitation to suffer with Jesus and walked away, I had no idea I would pass my pain on to my family.

> When I misunderstood the invitation to suffer with Jesus and walked away, I had no idea I would pass my pain on to my family.

By the grace of God, the very next day, a family and children's social worker showed up at our door. Our daughter Shaylea had gone to school and said I was a drug addict and alcoholic, that nobody loved her, we had no food, and she feared for her life. These allegations opened an investigation into our home where my addictive behaviors were brought to light, and the other claims were found to be false.

The family and children services' worker said I had one week to get into rehab or the kids were going to be taken away, even though my husband was sober and the other allegations were proven to be false. There was no fear for our children in our house.

God was stripping me of all my comforts. He was hedging me in and putting a wall in front of me that I could not get around.

That night, again only by God's grace, I was reconnected with Teresa, a friend from the church, whose husband I had gone to school with to become a pastor. She asked, "How are things?"

Usually I would have said fine, but that night I told her exactly where I was. I told her exactly what was happening, and the words appeared on the screen: "Well, Jenn, you could come here." I did not know what to say other than I would have to talk to Ken first because I did not know if we could afford it.

Isn't this just like God? Hosea 2:14–15 (NLT) says, "But then I will win her back once again. I will lead her into the desert and speak tenderly to her there. I will return her vineyards to her and transform the Valley of Trouble into a gateway of hope."

The Father knows the unique lifelines we each need to be able to grasp onto His hand. He led me to the desert, stripping me naked along the way.

Teresa's invitation was given to me at a time when I had to choose addiction or my family. Hands down, my family was first, but even before them, I had to choose me. Teresa's offer was my gateway to hope. Only God can orchestrate this.

When I found myself at the airport saying goodbye to my family, I didn't know exactly how long I would be gone—or even if this was going to work. I didn't even know that this was an actual answer to my husband's prayer. Nonetheless, with tears streaming down my face, I boarded the plane and headed off to Prince Edward Island.

Philippians 1:29 (NLT) says, "For you have been given not only the privilege of trusting in Christ but also the privilege of suffering for him."

It is in our humanness that we go back to what brings us comfort, whether it is good for us or not. Over the past eleven years, I have learned a great deal about suffering. I believe the reason suffering is such a privilege is when we allow God to enter into our pain, the communion that happens between us is so sweet. Jesus speaks tenderly, compassionately, and encourages me; He reveals things to me from His Word and through circumstances around me. He also sits with me while I cry. He holds me in ways that give me great assurance that He will never leave me nor forsake me. The more I suffer with Christ, the more I learn that my life is to be poured out for the Lord, and that includes the privilege of suffering.

> When we allow God to enter into our pain, the communion that happens between us is so sweet.

ᨒ Living Truth

For you have been given not only the privilege of trusting in Christ but also the privilege of suffering for him. (Philippians 1:29 NLT)

ᨒ Living Prayer

Father in heaven, thank You for the invitation to suffer with You. Not only do You invite us, but You call it a privilege. Lord, help us to see the privilege of suffering in our circumstances. Show us the truth in the pain You have for us. Keep us steadfast in You.

ᨒ Living Action

- Think of a personal time of suffering; how was God at work in your life?
- Do you see your suffering as a privilege? Why or why not?
- How does God comfort you in your suffering?

_____

_____

_____

_____

_____

_____

_____

Jenn Dafoe-Turner is a child of the King of Kings and Lord of Lords. She is a wife, mother, and Memaw. She lives in Ontario, Canada, with her husband Ken where she pastors a small Nazarene church with a big heart. She loves to journey and share Christ with those she meets.

Chapter Thirty

This Crazy-Wonderful Little Life
Sara Cormany

I remember the day he took my breath away.

It began like most appointments, I suppose. With my feet dangling over the side of an exam table, the nurse's fingers clickety-clacking away at the computer, and the doctor posing the question as he had many times before, "On a scale of one to ten, how is the pain here? And here? And here?"

A squeeze, a number, a clickety-clack. As this little routine ended, he asked, "Do you have any more questions?"

I answered playfully, "I don't know that I would remember even if I did!"

And then we all giggled at my short-term memory, because in hard things you must. Not long after, I started to shimmy to the floor, expecting the doctor's usual goodbye. But this time, he held his hand out as if to stop me and said, "How is your connective-tissue disease affecting your ability to be the mother of four?"

I answered with incredible eloquence, "Er . . . um . . ."

"No, really, Sara. I want to know."

I stared at my dangling feet, hoping I could muster something true, but all that came out was another giggle and, "Oh, you know, it makes it hard and hilarious and crazy messy, but kind of wonderful too . . ." Something in my eyes must have said that I couldn't say more because he pressed no further, the clickety-clack slowed to a stop, and we said goodbye.

I made it as far as my van before hot tears welled in my eyes. Sinking into the driver's seat, I sat in all the raw places his question opened. Counting each tear and crying out to the One who had seen every struggle, every fall, every fight.

Because even my bravest giggle cannot change the truth. I have a disease. One that is relentless and unkind. One that takes away new pieces of me every year and leaves me broken every day. One that demands my four babies and sweet man wade in all its messiness.

And it is hard.

Hard to find yourself in quiet corners, asking God the what-ifs and the whys, begging for grace every second because it is the only way you know how to breathe. Hard to hold on with white knuckles to every promise He speaks and every happy moment given. Hard to trust that all the hurt in their little hearts caused by your illness will grow into something beautiful and good. It is a daily battle for grace. One that asks us to let go of the outcome, the prognosis, the future, and trade it for the gift of today and the promise of forever.

And yet? Even in the hard, the crazy, the messy reality of a broken mama with four babies comes the part that is so immeasurably good. With every day that passes, I am given the gift and grace of watching the little turn into big. Be it little into big hands and hearts. Or little into big lives and dreams. Or little into big prayers and promises kept. All wrapped up in a love so sufficient it will not be bested by some measly little disease. All gathered in their mama's heart so no piece of them can be taken away. All bathed in a grace that comes in knowing there is no way without Jesus.

> I have a disease. One that is relentless and unkind. One that takes away new pieces of me every year and leaves me broken every day.

To deny such goodness would be to deny our very breath.

But on the days and in the things that try to break us, it can be hard to hear a melody of "Give thanks in all circumstances," because our humanity often chafes at the thought of being thankful for pain and hurt and the brokenness that comes with it. But it is in the chafing, in the refining, where we discover God's goodness is present even in the middle of our deepest suffering. Our pain, our brokenness, our sorrow doesn't change our God. It changes us by opening our eyes to His beauty in the madness. Even when a chapter of our story feels like a lifetime, we can hold tightly to a promise He makes. A promise Elisabeth Elliot so beautifully penned, "Of one thing I am certain, God's story never ends in ashes."[7]

And it is why when I've been asked the hard questions—the ones that nearly break me at their call for vulnerability—my heart always answers, I would never have chosen this disease, this path of brokenness. But I would choose the story He has written in it. Every single time, I would choose it. For it is in this sacred place where my hands uncurl to welcome the good Jesus gives in every curve and every line and every page of hurt and hard things.

Be it in the chance to know Him, permanently face-planted at His feet. Be it in the grace to love and mother differently, to stumble and fall, but to know He is in it. Or be it in the gift of little into big hands and hearts and faces reminding me of the beauty He brings from this often messy, tattered story.

It is a grace unmatchable. It is a blessing undeniable. It is a hope unstoppable. And it is why I will say until I find my way home (heaven), I am grateful for every single breath He gives in this crazy-wonderful little life.

Living Truth

Give thanks to the Lord for he is good; his love endures forever. (Psalm 107:1 NIV)

Jesus, hold our hands open to Your promises—the comfort of Your peace, the sufficiency of Your grace, and the healing power of Your hope. May we come to You in the good things, the hard things, and all the things in between with a trust built in who You are and what You have done in the work of the cross. May we find ourselves face-planted at Your feet, not because of the circumstance but because it is our favorite place to be. May we find gratitude for even the hard and tender places, holding fast to the mercy of a new morning and a place to live, to love, and to be loved by a God who intimately knows our hearts and our struggle. Amen.

```
I would never have
chosen this disease,
this path of brokenness.
But I would choose the
story He has written in
it. Every single time.
```

 *Living Action*

- What are the raw and tender places in your own story?
- How do you struggle with finding gratitude in those places?
- How can you invite God into your pain and pursue gratitude within that invitation?

_____

_____

_____

_____

_____

_____

_____

_____

_____

_____

_____

Sara Cormany loves to see the grace of God in the messiest of life. She is wife to one sweet guy and mom to four messy, beautiful kids. Her most recent book, *Born Beautiful*, guides moms and daughters through a God-breathed conversation on beauty and identity. And while most of her journey has been written through the lens of chronic and life-threatening illness, Sara is living proof a hard story can still be a good story. Connect with her on her Facebook or at saracormany.com.

Endnotes

1. Pam Farrel, *10 Best Decisions a Woman Can Make* (Eugene, OR: Harvest House, 1999), 65–67.
2. Candy Arrington and David Cox, *Aftershock: Help, Hope, and Healing in the Wake of Suicide* (Nashville: B & H Publishing, 2003).
3. Lyrics by Cheri Keaggy, "Destination Home."
4. Albert Y. Hsu, *Grieving a Suicide: A Loved One's Search for Comfort, Answers, and Hope* (Downer's Grove, IL: Intervarsity Press, 2017).
5. Ann Voskamp, *The Broken Way* (Grand Rapids, MI: Zondervan, 2016), 136.
6. L. B. Cowman, *Streams in the Desert* (Grand Rapids, MI: Zondervan, 1997), 279.
7. Elisabeth Elliot, *These Strange Ashes* (Grand Rapids: Revell, 2004).

Copyrights

She Writes for Him

ROMANS 8:28
B O O K S
AN IMPRINT OF REDEMPTION PRESS

To order additional copies of this book, please visit
www.redemption-press.com.
Also available on Amazon.com
or by calling toll-free 1-844-2REDEEM.

Other books in this series:
She Writes for Him: Stories of Resilient Faith
She Writes for Him: Black Voices of Wisdom

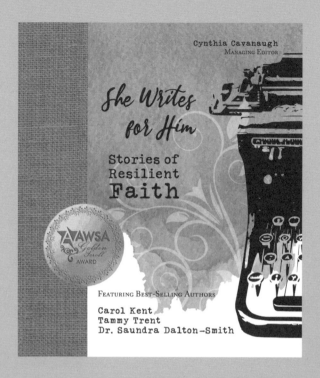

She Writes for Him: Stories of Resilient Faith is the debut book in the She Writes for Him Series and winner of the 2020 AWSA Golden Scroll Award.

Written by thirty brave women who have boldly ventured out to tell their hard stories believing God can be trusted in the midst of tragic circumstances. They found God's redemption through their pain and stories of abortion, shame, betrayal, depression, anxiety, and loss.

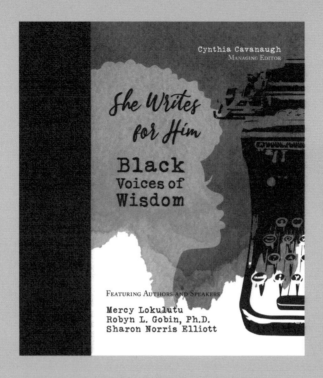

Twenty-one Black Christian women

share their powerful life experiences with racism in this vital compilation

that brings wisdom and new insight to the conversation on racial inequality

and justice. Each story includes prayer and reflection and is a tool for

building bridges of love and understanding.